Green Rûna

GREEN RÛNA

The Runemaster's Notebook:
Shorter Works of Edred Thorsson
Volume I
(1978-1985)

Third Edition

Lodestar
Historical Reprint

Copyright © 2021
Lodestar

All rights reserved. No part of this book, either in part or in whole, may be reproduced, transmitted or utilized in any form or by any means electronic, photographic or mechanical, including photocopying, recording, or by any information storage and retrieval system, without the permission in writing from the Publisher, except for brief quotations embodied in literary articles and reviews.

For permissions, or for the serialization, condensation, or for adaptation write the Publisher at the address below.

First Edition 1993
Second Improved and Expanded Edition, 1996

For List of Books Available from Lodestar:
www.seekthemysteries.com

Published by Lodestar
Email:
tilruna72@gmail.com

Table of Contents

Preface vii

Runelore
What is a "Rune"? (1980) 1
The Fuþark (1981) 3
The Elder or the Younger Fuþark? (1983) 7
Holy Signs I: Three-fold (1983) 9
Holy Signs II: Four-fold (1984) 12
The Use of Holy Signs in Rune-work (1984) 15
A Curious Curse Formula (1983) 16
The Rune-Lore of Kylver, Gotland's Fuþark Stone (1982) 17
The Uthark Theory and the Tarot (1982) 18

Germanic Studies
Reincarnation in Ásatrú (1979) 25
"Fate" in Ásatrú (1980) 28
The Sumble (1979) 30
Ancient Foundations of the Rune-cult in Europe (1981) 32
I, the Runemaster (1981) 35
Hidden God-lore: Are the Gods Our Ancestors? (1984) 37
Euhemerism in Ásatrú (1985) 39
The Holy (1982) 41
A Rune of Huginn (1985) 46
An English Runo-Wôdenic Survival in the Middle Ages (1983) 49
More on the Liége Wôden-page (1983) 51
Rune-Wisdom and Race (1982) 53
A Brief History of German Runic Esotericism (1982) 59
The *Armanenschaft* (1982) 62
Personal Authority and Odian Ethics (1980) 64
Languages (1985) 67

Reviews
Carlyle Pushong. *Rune Magic*. (1979) 73
Thorsteinn Gudjónsson. *Astrobiology: The Science of the
    Universe*. (1982) 74
Haack, Friedrich-Wilhelm. *Wotans Wiederkehr: Blut-Boden-und-
    Rasse Religion* (1982) 75
Mund, Rudolf J. *Jörg Lanz von Liebenfels und der Neue
    Templer Orden: die Esoterik des
    Christentums* (1982) 76
Hans F. Günter. *The Religious Attitudes of the Indo-
    Europeans* (1983) 78
Marijane Osborn and Stella Longland. *Rune Games*. (1983) 79

Appendices
Appendix A: The Awakening of a Runemaster:
    The Life of Edred Thorsson by James Allen Chisholm 81
Appendix B: Introductory Information:
    The Outer Hall of the Rune-Gild 90
Appendix C: Information on the Rune-Gild
    Valid after Midsummer 1990 93
Glossary 95
Bibliography 96

Acknowledgments

Thanks go to my wife Crystal Dawn for her supportive work at Rûna-Raven Press. And a very special note of thanks to Dianne Ross who helped prepare the original typescript of this collection.

Preface

Often the written works produced for rather obscure journals or newsletters are lost over time because the journals themselves are not preserved. This collection brings Edred's early works to a wider readership than ever had a chance to read them before. Many of these articles and reviews give insight into *Futhark, Runelore* and his other well-known published works.

The idea of calling this volume "Green Rûna" is an indication that the material contained in it is rather "unripe." But it is still valuable fruit.

All of the articles printed here are headed with indications of their original publication data. *The Runestone* was the official publication of the Ásatrú Free Assembly from 1973 to the demise of that organization in 1987. *Raven Banner* was the official organ of the Committee for the Restoration of the Odinic Rite. *Rûna* was the official publication of the Rune-Gild from 1980 to 1984, which was replaced by *New Rûna*, only four volumes of which were published in 1985.

Edred also plans to release his shorter works (often for more visible journals) between 1985 and the present (to be called *Red Rûna*), and more intriguingly, a select volume of his shorter works written for publications within the Order of the Trapezoid— which will be called *Black Rûna*.

For the most part these offerings stand as they were originally written. Some corrections of fact and references to later works have been made on occasion. But for the most part the reader sees these articles as they first appeared in various Troth-journals. When referring to the Troth, these texts almost always use the terms "Ásatrú" or "Odinism." These reflected the usage of the day. Now those terms would simply be replaced with the straightforward term *Troth*.

James A. Chisholm
Austin, Texas 1993

Reyn til Rúna!

Abbreviations

BCE	Before the Common Era (= BC)
CE	Common Era (= AD)
Go.	Gothic
IE	Indo-European
OE	Old English
OFris.	Old Frisian
OHG	Old High German
ON	Old Norse
OS	Old Saxon
PGmc.	Proto-Germanic
PIE	Proto-Indo-European
pl.	plural
sg.	singular
st.	stanza
sts.	stanzas

Notes on Special Characters

Special Germanic printed characters are used in this book. The "thorn" (þ) generally has the sound of a voiceless "th" (as in the modern English "thin." The "edh" (ð) generally has the sound of the voiced "th" (as in the modern English "than." This latter character was often transliterated as "dh" in other publications.

Runic characters are transcribed by boldface Roman characters throughout.

Part I
RUNELORE

WHAT IS A "RUNE"?
(From *The Runestone*, No. 34, Winter, 1980)

Before we may begin to understand the runic system we must first discover the true and most basic meanings of the individual runes, and in order to do this, the true and deep level meaning of the concept "rune" must be determined.

"Rune" has by now become synonymous with "letter," but this is hardly accurate. Originally, the two concepts had nothing in common. The etymology of the word is difficult. It is perhaps connected to Proto-Indo-European *reu-: "to bellow, roar," but the term is really only common to the Germanic and Celtic dialects, and is more probably derived from a Proto-Germanic form *rûnô-: "mystery, secret" as a technical term in the culto-magical field.

In any event, this latter meaning of "mystery" is reflected in all the attested dialects and is indeed the original significance of the word. It is found in the Old Norse *rún*: "secret, wisdom; magical sign; written character," Gothic *rûna*: "mystery," Old English *rûn*: "mystery, secret council," Old Saxon *rûna*: "mystery, secret," Old High German *rûna*: "mystery." The root also occurs in Old Irish *rún*: "mystery," and in Middle Welsh *rhîn*: "mystery, secret."

The Finnish word *runo*, "a magic song, stanza," was not borrowed from *rûnô*, but from Germanic *runo*, which meant a "row" or *series* of things.

Our new English word "rune" is not a direct genetic descendent from the Old English *rûn*, but rather a borrowing from 17th century scholarly Latin which had borrowed it from Germanic.

The semantic transition from "mystery" to "letter" is not too difficult to understand. The mysteries, and secret lore, came to be symbolized by certain ideographic signs, and when these were later systemized and used as a form of writing, the technical term came to be used for both the sign and the thing symbolized by the sign.

With this basic foundation, we may now explore the deeper levels of meaning to be found in the complex concept "rune." From an early time each runic sign had a particular numerical value which it held by virtue of its position in a definite runic order. It also had a special name, a certain shape, a phonetic value, and a whole set of ideas which were attached to this complex. These characteristics may be arranged in a three-fold structure:

  I. Content: ideological significance
  II. Form: stave-shape and phonetic value
  III. Context: number and order in a rune-row

In order to begin to understand what a rune is, one must always keep all of these aspects in mind simultaneously.

Runes exist in all realms of being at all times, they exist within the human psychophysical complex and in the multiverse, or world. In fact, the runic correspondences between these (apparently) distinct realms constitute one of the great runes. The runes distinguish between "this" and "that," but at the same time they form bridges between the two. All things "have their runes," i.e. their essential secrets or mysteries which lie behind their appearances— and appearances are often deceiving. Through an interaction of the world-runes and the man-runes (those of the human psychophysical complex), the rune-*vitki* ("runic magician," or "wise one") is able to first gain knowledge, and then use that knowledge in accordance with the wisdom gained, to become a more potent force in the world.

Each rune is a dynamic force unto itself, yet it exists within a tightly woven ecosystem of energy. What is most useful to keep in mind about the runes is their multiple aspects with an integrated model of wholeness, and to see the runic sign-sound as a key that unlocks a whole rune.

The runic system provides us with an indigenous, symbolic meta-language with which we can explore ourselves and the multiverse, express our experiences, and indeed shape our consciousness. Such an indwelling meta-language is an invaluable tool in the emergence of Ásatrú— but as with all "languages" one must learn to speak, to understand, to read, and to write before one may effectively use the language.

THE FUÞARK
(From *The Runestone*, No. 35, Spring, 1981)

In this article we propose to discuss the nature of the fuþark system and its historical manifestations. The word "fuþark" is the invention of 19th century scholars, and it is an acronym formed from the phonetic values of the first six staves of the rune-row (see below). However, the principle of having the first few staves magically stand for the entire row was one used in ancient times as well. Part of the inscription on the 6th century bow brooch of Aquincum reads:

Under no circumstances should it be forgotten that the term "rune" is a complex one, with the primary definition of "mysterium, arcanum, secret lore," and only secondarily the sign or symbol of that particle or unit of the great hidden network which constitutes the secret traditions of the ancient Germanic peoples.

The runic system is a complex of factors, all of which inter-relate to form a living, organic structure. The basic ingredients in this structure are:

    I. Name (phonetic value and idea)
    II. Shape
    III. Order (number)
    IV. Triplicy

That is, each runestave has a distinctive name which conveys a kernel concept in the runic ideology— while the first phoneme in the name indicates the phonetic value of the stave in writing practice. It must also be borne in mind that the staves were often used as ideograms as well. j could stand for the concept "good harvest," as well as for the sound [j] (pronounced as in English /y/). The shape of the stave is also ideographic, and imparts a vast teaching to the unconscious realms of the human psyche (*hugr*). The ordering of the staves (and the resulting numerical values) constitute the first element of the inter-runic network. Through number, connections are revealed and bonds can be made. The next level of the inter-runic network is expressed by the division of the fuþark system into three sets called *ættir* (sg. *ætt*: "family, kindred" in Old Norse.) This too communicates a new set of connections and makes a new level of bond-shaping possible.

As can be seen from the various fuþark systems outlined below, there is a remarkable level of consistency in these factors. It can scarcely be doubted that a great tradition underlies the systematic consistency of these factors over at least a thousand years of Odian rune-lore. There are essentially two great historical periods for the runic tradition: the "elder" and the "younger." The period of the Elder Fuþark of 24 staves spans from at least 150 to around 750 CE (although runestaves continued to be used in writing and magic well into the 19th century). The first great runic revival was effected by Guido von List when he formulated the somewhat non-traditional Armanen Futhork in the first decade of this century. This latter system can not be ignored in any discussion of runic history due to its influence on exoteric and esoteric world history, and because of its status in present day Germany. We will now enter upon schematic outlines of the various fuþark systems for future reference and study.

Regardless of later expressions and/or modifications, the Elder Fuþark remains the standard of esoteric runic studies. One of the simpler reasons for this is the fact that the magico-religious Odian cult was most vigorous in this period.

Knowledge of the following outlines is the beginning of rune-wisdom. Here the various fuþarks are given in their ætt-systems with numerical and phonetic values, and are followed by a list of their names and the English meanings of those names.

Elder Fuþark

1(f)	2(u)	3(þ)	4(a)	5(r)	6(k)	7(g)	8(w)
9(h)	10(n)	11(i)	12(j)	13(ï)	14(p)	15(z)	16(s)
17(t)	18(b)	19(e)	20(m)	21(l)	22(ng)	23(d)	24(o)

(1) *fehu*: "livestock, money," (2) *úruz*: "aurochs," (3) *þurisaz*: "the strong one," (4) *ansuz*: "a god," (5) *raiðô*: "wagon," (6) *kênaz*: "torch," (7) *gebô*: "gift," (8) *wunjô*:: "joy," (9) *hagalaz*: "hail," (10) *nauðiz*: "need," (11) *îsa*: "ice," (12) *jêra*: "year," (13) *eihwaz*: "yew," (14) *perþrô*:: "dice box" (?), (15) *elhaz*: "elk"-or- *algiz* "protection," (16) *sowilô*:: "sun," (17) *teiwaz*: "the god Týr," (18) *berkanô*: "the birch goddess," (19) *ehwaz*: "horse," (20) *mannaz*: "human," (21) *laguz*: "water," (22) *ingwaz*: "the god Ing," (23) *dagaz*: "day," (24) *ôþala*: "ancestral property."

Generally, the Old English row follows that of the Elder Fuþark, with an extension of the tow by eventually nine staves to make a total of 33 staves. This is the usual pattern of alphabetic modification to accommodate linguistic change.

Old English Futhorc

1(f)	2(u)	3(þ)	4(o)	5(r)	6(c)	7(g)	8(w)
9(h)	10(n)	11(i)	12(g)	13(ë)	14(p)	15(x)	16(s)
17(t)	18(b)	19(e)	20(m)	21(l)	22(ng)	23(d)	24(œ)
25(a)	26(æ)	27(y)	28(êa)	29(eo)	30(q)	31(k)	32(st)	33(g)

(1) *feoh*: "cattle, money," (2) *ûr*: "ox," (3) *þorn*: "thorn," (4) *ôs*: "a god," (5) *râd*: "riding," (6) *cên*: "torch," (7) *gyfu*: "gift," (8) *wynn*: "pleasure," (9) *hægl*: "hail," (10) *nɨd*: "need," (11) *îs*: "ice," (12) *gêr*: "year," (13) *eoh*: "yew," (14) *peorþ*: "chess-man," (?) (15) *eolh*: "elk," (16) *sigil*: "sun," (17) *tîr*: "the god Tîw" - or - "glory," (18) *beorc*: "birch," (19) *eh*: "horse," (20) *mann*: "human," (21) *lagu*: "water," (22) *ing*: "the god Ing," (23) *dæg*: "day," (24) *œþel*: "ancestral property," (25) *âc*: "oak," (26) *æsc*: "ash," (27) *yr*: "gold decoration," (28) *ior*: "serpent," (29) *êar*: "earth-grave," (30) *cweorþ*: "fire-twirl," (31) *calc*: "cup," (32) *stân*: "stone," (33) *gâr*: "spear."

What is especially noteworthy about the Younger Fuþark is that although there was a similar level of linguistic change in the Scandinavian dialects, as in the Ingvaeonic (Old English, Old Frisian, etc., which made use of the previous Futhorc), it was not expanded as would have been expected, but rather contracted along consistent, systematic, and traditional guidelines. The *ætt*-system became even more vigorously represented in the Viking Age.

(Note that each *ætt* begins with the same stave as in the elder period.)

Younger Fuþark

ᚠ	ᚢ	ᚦ	ᚨ	ᚱ	ᚴ
1(f)	2(u/o)	3(þ)	4(a)	5(r)	6(k/g)

ᚼ	ᚾ	ᛁ	ᛅ	ᛋ
7(h)	8(n)	9(i/e)	10(a)	11(s)

ᛏ	ᛒ	ᛘ	ᛚ	ᛦ
12(t/d)	13(b/p)	14(m)	15(l)	16(-R)

(1) *fé*: "livestock; money," (2) *úr*: "drizzle" -or- "slag," (3) *þurs*: "giant," (4) *áss*: "a god," (5) *reið*: "riding," (6) *kaun*: "sore," (7) *hagall*: "hail," (8) *nauþ*: "need," (9) *íss*: "ice," (10) *ár*: "(good) year," (11) *sól*: "sun," (12) *Tɨr*: "the god Tɨr," (13) *bjarkan*: "runic birch goddess," (14) *maðr*: "man," (15) *lögr* "water," (16) *ɨr*: "yew."

Here we have looked at the ancient forms of the fuþark, but no discussion would be complete without an outline of the Armanen system of Guido von List. This system is a modification and expansion of the Younger Fuþark based upon the 18 runic stanzas of the *rúnaþáttr* of the "Hávamál" (138-165). This version was first published by von List in his book *Das Geheimnis der Runen* (1908).

Armanen Futhork

ᛒ	ᚢ	ᚦ	ᚭ	ᚱ	ᚴ	ᚼ	ᚾ	ᛁ
1(f)	2(u)	3(th)	4(o)	5(r)	6(k)	7(h)	8(n)	9(i)

ᛅ	ᛋ	ᛏ	ᛒ	ᛚ	ᛘ	ᛦ	ᛂ	ᚵ
10(a)	11(s)	12(t)	13(b)	14(l)	15(m)	16(y)	17(e)	18(g)

The names of the runes are based upon the historical ones, but have an esoteric significance peculiar to List's system. (1) Fa, (2) Ur, (3) Thorn, (4) Os, (5) Rit, (6) Ka, (7) Hagal, (8) Not, (9) Is, (10) Ar, (11) Sig, (12) Tyr, (13) Bar, (14) Laf, (15) Man, (16) Yr, (17) eh, (18) Gibor.

THE ELDER OR THE YOUNGER FUÞARK?
(From *Rúna*, Vol. I, No. 2, Walburga, 1983)

In a fine essay response to the work of *Lore-Book* I in the old IRSA course-work, a fellow of the Workshop expressed the idea that the younger fuþark of 16 runes seemed more suitable for esoteric work than that of the elder system of 24 runes. The question of which to use has for the most part been a closed one in Vinland— since most runesters, even working independently, have come to the inner conclusion that the 24-rune system is somehow "right." For my own part, I have always contended that from an overall point of view, the 16-rune fuþark is just as legitimate as that of the 24-rune system for esoteric work. This is principally because the 16-rune system grew organically from the 24-rune system under the direction of an integral, if historically ephemeral, network or gild of runemasters around 800 CE. We know that there is a traditional continuity between the elder and younger rows because the latter retains systematic features (names, division of the row into three groups) from the elder period. Because this new tradition became quickly codified and enforced throughout the Scandinavian territory, we can also see that the old gild was still at work setting the standards across tribal boundaries.

A quick look at the systematic relationship between the two rows shows that those who codified the 16-rune system knew well the elder row (we also have epigraphical evidence on the famous Rök stone [about 850 CE] where elder runes are used alongside younger ones).

```
ᚠᚢᚦᚨᚱ  <ᚲᚷᚹ:ᚺ  ᛀᛁ ᚻᛃᛈᛉᛇ ᛉ:ᛏᛒ  ᛗᛘᛚ•  ᛜ ᛟ
f u þ a r   k g w  h  n i j ï p z s  t b  e m l ng  d o
                           |
                           |
                        ---+----------------------→

ᚠᚢᚦᚨᚱ ᚱ     :ᚺ ᛀᛁ ᛉ        ᛊ:ᛏᛒ    ᛘ ᛚ             ᛦ
f u þ a r k      h  n i a     s t b     m l            R
```

Beyond this formal relationship, there is also a condensation of the integrated lore— although that must be the subject of another study— many of the relationships in the esoteric lore can be understood through the formal transformations.

One of the most useful aspects of the younger row is its historical and mytho-systematic unity with the world of the Eddas and sagas in Old Norse literature. So that if we were to use a system of runic analysis for these works, it would be the 16-rune system which would be most suited to the task. However, it is also clear that 24-foldness continued to be important in the Viking Age— see the 24 things upon which runes are to be carved in the "Sigdrífumál" sts. 17-19.

The chief attraction of the elder system from an objective viewpoint is that the separate runes (that is, mysteries in contrast to the staves which are a part of them) are more clearly delineated in what is certainly the archetypal (Indo-European) configuration of 24-foldness ($3 \times 8 = 2 \times 12 = 24$— the number of the roads between the 9 Worlds of Yggdrasill)— also the number arrived at by the Greeks in their cosmological alphabetic formulations. This has the added quality of being pan-Germanic— having been a system common to all Germanic tribes it is deeply impressed into the archetypal realms and is now most suitable for re-emergence in the tribally pluralistic societies of Vinland and Britain— although both are essentially founded on the Anglo-Saxon mind.

The 18 "runic" stanzas of the "Rúnaþáttr Óðins" ("Hávamál" sts. 138-164) were also brought into play by the aforementioned respondent— something which was also done by *der Meister* Guido von List. This results in the (unattested) 18-rune futhork— which is now the occult establishment in Germany among the Armanen. List, of course, saw the 18-rune futhork as the archetypal one (with its origins in Thule/Atlantis)— while others might see it as a two rune (re-)extension of the 16-rune fuþark.

The Armanen Futhork

FA	UR	THORN	OS	RIT	KA	HAGAL	NOT	IS
AR	SIG	TYR	BAR	LAF	MAN	YR	EH	GIBOR

From a historical perspective, the problems with the 18-rune system are, 1) there is no existing inscription which uses the system (for example, the forms for AR and SIG are taken from medieval manuscript runes), and 2) we do not know for sure that the 18 stanzas of the "Rúnaþáttr" refer to rune-staves at all. There, the word "rune" (ON *rún*) may mean more "magical incantation," or have its more generic meaning "mystery, lore"— and this would then be a listing of magical songs and not rune-staves. A similar tradition may be found in both the "Sigrdrífumál" and in the "Gróagaldr" (see Lee M. Hollander *The Poetic Edda*.) This is not to say that runic correspondences can not be made— this is a part of the rune poem work in *Runelore* (Weiser 1987).

To sum up, it seems that for the work of the gild the 24-rune system is best suited — although we should actively engage in work within the 16-rune system and develop its lore — because of its genetic relationship to the elder system, and its organic integrity with the vast mythic lore of the Eddas and sagas. Local groups within Ásatrú/Odinism or individuals who wish to emphasize the Scandinavian focus within the greater Germanic context may indeed prefer the 16-rune row.

The idea that the Younger Fuþark reflects a stage in the evolution of consciousness in the North is an intriguing one— and one which bears further research. At this point in our researches, however, it seems that the younger row represents a contraction of the quantity (but not the quality or essence) of the mysteries. This reform of the fuþark certainly demonstrates that the system was in the control of conscious forces of a special kind, since the reduction of a graphemic system in response to an increase in phonetic complexity is contrary to usual alphabetic history. This could have only been carried out by conscious forces — a self-conscious network of human beings — with extra-linguistic considerations. Also, if the runic record itself is any indicator (and what better direct source do we have?), the possible evolution would have been from a more magical world-view toward a more rational, objective one, since although the number of inscriptions radically increases, the number of overtly magical ones drops significantly.

HOLY SIGNS I: THREE-FOLD
(From *Rúna*, Vol. 1, no. 3, Midsummer, 1983)

The study of ideographic signs is a complex one in Germanic lore. Ideographic signs are distinguished from rune staves in that they 1) do not have phonetic values and 2) can have extremely complex forms. They are similar to runes in that they often have special names and, of course, have an "ideological" content— th.i. they express whole and usually multiformed concepts. Since this "idea" is a religio-magical one, we can call these signs holy (full of sacred power). These holy signs are of many different types in Germanic lore— some of the most archaic ones may be classified according to numerical formulas, that is, they are based on three-foldedness, four-foldedness, and so forth. Other later signs, called *galdrastafir* or *galdramyndir* in Old Icelandic, are sometimes inspired by models found in Continental magical grimoires— but with definite Nordic input. Here is an example of such a *galdramynd* taken from the infamous Kreddur manuscripts of the Icelandic magician Jón *lærdi* ("the learned") who lived between 1574 and ab. 1650:

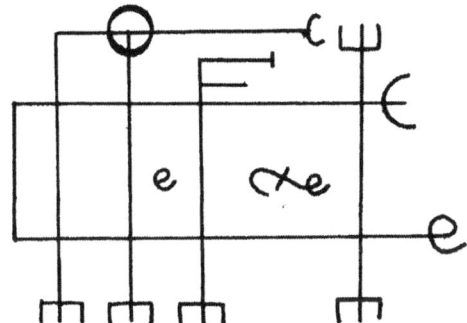

This symbol bears the explanatory text: "Have this sign in your right hand against the fear of magic." This type of sign and magic is to be the subject of my work entitled *The Galdrabók: An Icelandic Grimoire* (Weiser, 1989) and is also treated in my book *Northern Magic* (Llewellyn, 1991).

What we want to explore here, however, are the more archaic — and somewhat more familiar — holy signs. In this article we will consider the triplectic or three-fold signs.

The triplectic signs, those emphasizing the number three, are by far the most vigorous and varied of the ideographic types on Germanic artifacts. In the symbolism of old Germanic religion, the number three is quite prominent— the three Nornir, numerous triads of gods, the tripartite cultic drinking rites, the use of three in rites of divination, the three "roots" of Yggdrasill, and perhaps most importantly, the three great sacrificial festivals at Vetrnætr, Jól, and Midsumar. All point to a cosmic, yet organic, significance for the number three in Germanic symbology. It is a cyclical symbol, as well as one of verticality, see the three "roots" (here used in a metaphorical sense) of Yggdrasill which connect the under-world with that of the gods and men (*Prose Edda, Gylfaginning*, ch. 15). The iconography of the common three-fold signs shares in all the symbolic content of the complex symbology.

The unique triquetra opens the doors to a very
specific interpretation. This sign is called the *valknútr*
"knot of the fallen" in Old Norse, and it occurs
consistently in connection with a horse or horse and
rider. The cursive type certainly gives the impression of
a magical knot. This fits quite well with the Odinic
power of binding his enemies and of unfettering his
heroes. The *valknútr* is a sign of Óðinn's power over
life and death, over liberation and bondage, therefore it is closely
connected with the rites and symbolism of death and shamanism.

A special type of the *valknútr* is the angular type
which emphasizes the numerical formula $3 \times 3 = 9$,
through the representation of three triangles interlocked
in one form. The number nine, along with three, is the
most potent number in Ásatrú numerology. Nine is
sometimes used as a formulaic amplification of three,
e.g. the multiplication of the three by three non-human
races— the Æsir, *álfar*, and *dvergar* ("Fáfnismál" 13).
Nine is most often connected to concepts of birth, death, and re-birth in
the cosmos, and among men and gods— usually in the context of Odinic
aspects.

To gain runic wisdom, Óðinn hangs for nine nights
("Hávamál" 138-39) on the World-Tree, which is made
up of nine worlds ("Völuspá" 2). He is then taught
nine magical songs by his maternal uncle ("Hávamál"
140). Some other uses of nine would include: the ring
Draupnir, which reproduces itself eight times every
ninth day ("Skírnismál" 21); the god Heimdall (who has
been identified with Óðinn) is said to be the son of
nine mothers; and the great sacrifice at Uppsala took place every nine
years, at which time for nine days, nine living beings from nine species
were sacrificed (Adam of Bremen, *Gesta Hammaburgensis Ecclesiae
Pontificum*: IV, 26-27). This Nordic form of the triquetra can be seen as
a direct reference to the Odinic cultus, and as a sign of the powers of
binding and release, death and birth, and thus the power of the dead
and of the shaman (*seiðmaðr/seiðkona*) to transverse the worlds.

Another triplectic sign unique to the North is that of the three
interlocked horns. While the *valknútr* can best be interpreted according to
numerical formulas, Óðinn's use of knots, etc., the interlocking horns may
be seen in a very specific mythic setting.

In both the "Hávamál" (104-110) and in the *Prose Edda* (*Skaldskaparmál*,
ch. I), we read about how Óðinn, in order to recover the poetic mead of
inspiration, bored his way into a mountain while in the shape of a
serpent. The etin-wife (giantess), Gunnlöð, dwelled in the mountain where
she kept the mead in three vessels called Óðrœrir ("exciter of inspiration"),
Boðn ("container") and Són ("compensatory sacrifice"). He sleeps with her
for three nights and she allows him to drink three draughts of the mead.
Óðinn empties the contents of all three vessels in three gulps, turns
himself into an eagle, and flies back to Ásgarðr, where he regurgitates the
mead into three vats. The poetic mead is a magical substance of
inspiration and something necessary to the life of men and of the gods.

These three interlocked drinking horns, arranged in a triquetra-like form, are certainly a magical sign of Óðinn and of his cult. This is especially clear when we remember the meaning of the god's name: "the ruler of inspiration"— and see this in connection with the main vessel which holds the poetic mead— *Óðrœrir*: "exciter of *óðr* (= inspiration)."

Probably more ancient, and certainly more widespread, is another three-fold sign— the triskelion. This sign, most widely known by its New Latin name [derived from a Greek original], is also the central theme of Celtic symbology, and is even an important sign to what John Yeowell has called the sister religion of Odinism— Shinto. In Japanese Shinto, it has the name *tomoë* and is said to be a special Japanese re-interpretation of the Taoist yin/yang. The trifos (as Guido von List called it) is an expression of the three-foldedness of the cosmos. By about 500 CE the symbol in this form had fallen into disuse— in favor of the *valknútr*.

HOLY SIGNS II: FOUR-FOLD
(From *Rúna*, Vol. I, no. 1, Midsummer, 1984)

In the previous essay we examined the triplectic signs — and their multiples — within Germanic symbology. Here we will delve into the quadraplectic holy signs based on a four-fold pattern. This type of symbol is more universal; that is, it is found among more different cultures of the world. The well known, almost universal, distribution of the swastika — represented on both sides of the Atlantic at very archaic stages of pre-history — is the most striking example.

The symbology of four-foldedness must be extended to the multiples of four in the progression 4-8-16-24, and so forth. This gives the basic key to a variety of more complex symbol structures. It must be pointed out that a similar progression is manifest in the analysis of the triplectic signs, that is, 3-6-12-15-18-21-24, and so forth. (Note that the point at which the four-fold progression meets the three-fold is at 24— the sacrosanct number.)

As a basic meaning of three-foldedness is vertical inter-connection (Asgard-Midgard-Hel) the underlying significance of four-foldedness is horizontal or lateral interconnection on the various fields of reality:

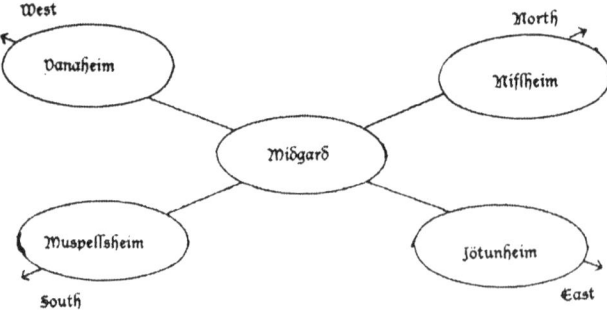

The dynamism of three is balanced by the stasis of four. But this stasis is only apparent from the outside. Within there is a dynamic interchange. The combination of these factors gives the four-fold entity an awesome power which makes it at once as hard as rock or steel from without and rush with the might and main of the wind within. This dichotomy of essence is apparent when we think deeply about the things symbolized by four-fold signs, such as the sun, the earth, Þórr's hammer, the helm of awe, and so forth.

It is most usual for symbols of Midgard to be four-fold signs. (But this is also generally true of the symbolism of any of the individual Worlds because of the effect of "localizing within or upon a plane" that the + sign has.) However, the simple + or ⊕ is not only a sign of Midgard in a cosmological sense, but it is also a sign of the hallowed stead, the cultic site used for sacrificial and juridical rites. Walter Blachetta, in his *Buch der deutschen Sinnzeichen* reports a bit of folklore concerning these type of crosses:

The *Sühnekreuz* is the sign for a divine stead or for a hallowed place and stands for reverence and veneration. On old country roads or also in the middle of fields we sometimes notice these stone crosses or field-stones into which these such crosses are carved. Present-day folklore usually has something to say about a crime (robbery and murder), that was supposed to have taken place on that spot many years before. It is for this reason that these crosses also bear the name "sin- or murder-crosses." There is, however, also the supposition that the `sin-crosses' actually originated in Germanic times and that they indicated heathen cultic sites, and that the present name and the murder stories were usually invented by the Church.

Quadraplectic signs are also most commonly used as symbols of the sky, sun, and lightning. From the most ancient times the sun-wheel (ON *sólarhvel*) has been used as a symbol for the sun. This sign is most prevalent on Northern Bronze Age rock carvings, and it seems to have been the most important single sign in their iconography.

Perhaps conceived of as a more dynamic version of this sign (and also called sólarhvel in Old Norse) is the "swastika." The ancient Indian designation *sv-asti-ka*: "a sign of well-being, or of good fortune," may well give us an archaic functional meaning for the sign. But especially in the North it was also a symbol of thunder and lightning and known as the *Þórshamarr* ("the hammer of Þórr"). It seems to have been a sign of the god, and of the traditional Norse religion when it came into conflict with Christianity. In the iconography of the runestones (especially the Swedish ones) we often find the *Þórshamarr* carved in the middle of an equilateral cross. The exact meaning of this composite symbol is problematic. It is usually assumed that the cross itself is Christian. The *Þórshamarr*, if it was originally part of the design may be a graphic manifestation of "blended troth" (a well-known condition); however, it is also possible that the swastika was carved to "de-Christianize" the stone. A third possibility remains that the whole is of heathen origin— "thunder and lightning in Midgard." It was apparently a Christian practice to go about carving crosses on runestones to "Christianize" them. This is directly referred to in

the curse formula of the Saleby stone: Old Swedish— *Werði at rata auk at argRi kunu, saR es håggwi krus, hwâ's of briuti*: "He will turn into a wretch and into a perverse woman, whoever carves a cross (into this monument), (or) whoever breaks it down!"

In much later times, a curious four-fold sign was used which seems to be a swastika more stylized to resemble a hammer. This "Hammer of Þórr" was a magical sign and used in magical operations.

An enticing bit of swastika-lore appeared in *Omni* magazine in July, 1983 (p. 102). There it was reported that two scientists as the University of Texas conducted an experiment in which hydrogen gas was exposed to electricity and magnetism: "At first the charged gas glowed ... then ... it parted to form the silhouette of a swastika." According to this article, "the researchers were led to speculate that the gaseous tail of a comet passing through the earth's magnetic field might cause a similar phenomenon, creating a swastika symbol in the sky." It must be noted, however, that when the researchers were questioned by a reporter from the *Daily Texan* (the student newspaper at the University of Texas) they denied that this observation and speculation had been made.

In Germanic symbology the quadraplectic signs encompass important cosmological concepts— of the definition of a field or plane of reality (a "world"), and a central location within it; of the sun (being a central part of one of these fields), and of the earth being another one within Midgard; but also of the expanse of the dome of the sky (actually another "shining plane"); and finally of that dynamic spark of force which streams from the heavens to the earth— of lightning.

The quadraplectic sign is a symbol of internal dynamism. From the outside it appears static, with a hard surface. But within it is a whirling dynamo. It shares this characteristic with the six-fold hagall-star ... which is, after all, a four-fold cross defining a horizontal plane intersected by a vertical column.

THE USE OF HOLY SIGNS IN RUNE-WORK
(From Rúna, Vol. I, No. 1, Midsummer, 1984)

The ways in which holy signs may be employed in rune-work are manifold. They may be used to analyze runes or other holy signs— what configurations are used to build up what kind of sign or rune? Once basic triplectic or quadraplectic patterns have been identified, and understood, their combinations will show special hidden qualities. They can be used in this manner in meditative practices, or they can constitute special mental states which are signified by the symbols. In "magic" — or rune-craft — their uses are also apparent. Triplectic signs would be used in workings of an externally dynamic, internally static nature— for example, the projection of the will to cause some effect in the environment. The effect is one of an evolutionary, non-violent nature— a gradual, progressive development. At the same time, the will of the being doing the work will be steadied and centered.

Quadraplectic signs have another function. They are externally static and internally dynamic. Their effect on the environment can be nil — if not projected — or it can have the violent and direct effect of displacement and destruction if projected by the will. The will of the projector is kept in a state of flux and change — internally evolutionary — but never chaotic.

Both signs give a center and focus for the will, and both have the power of setting evolutionary forces in motion. The effects of the triplectic signs, besides being externally dynamic are also vertically dynamic (that is, active in the vertical Asgard-Midgard-Hel axis), while quadraplectic signs are most active on the horizontal plane (for example, in the horizontal plane surrounding Midgard).

All of these factors should be taken into account when constructing ritual symbolism and giving shape to your thoughts. These are the roadways by which symbolism is deepened and broadened, and thereby given greater power.

A CURIOUS CURSE FORMULA
(From *Rúna*, Vol. I, No. 2, Walburga 1983)

While on the topics of later Anglo-Saxon traditions and the use of the Younger Fuþark, it is convenient to introduce an unusual inscription from Sutton, Cambridgeshire. It is on the back of a silver disk brooch (diam. 6') from the time between ab. 950-1050 CE. The main text runs around the back perimeter in Roman letters (Anglo-Saxon capitals) and it reads:

+ ÆDV EN MEAG AGE HUO DRIHTEN DRIHTEN HINE AÞERIE DEME
HIRE ÆTFERIE BVTON HYO ME SELLE HIRE AGENES ÞILLES

This is to be translated: "Æduwen owns me (the brooch) may the lord (*drihten*) own her. May the lord curse him who takes me from her, unless she gives me of her own will."

Two matters of vocabulary are interesting to note: 1) the well-known use of drihten (originally a term applied to lords of the retinue and to Anglo-Saxon priests) apparently for the Christian "lord," and 2) the word for "to curse"— *werian* (here in the subjunctive: (*w*)*erie*: "may he curse."). This latter term is a late OE form of *wyrgan*: "to curse," which originally had the sense— "to strangle" (and which is cognate to Modern English "to worry"— that is, "he worried him to death").

Besides this text, there is a second, fragmentary, cryptic and rune-like text on a pin-plate. All that remains is seven figures:

These have not been deciphered with any certainty. The signs seem to be based on the Younger Fuþark.

In addition to these two texts, there also appear two Anglo-Saxon forms of the *valknútr* (triquetra): carved on the inner surface area. This would be a prime example of the use of holy signs or ideographs to re-enforce the message of the syntactic and semantic text. The "knot of the slain" is a sign of Óðinn in several aspects (we will devote future work to the Germanic holy signs)— but here it indicates the closing noose of the God of Fetters and of the God of the Hanged as his bonds tighten around the potential victim of the curse. At least that is what it would have meant to the pre-Christian form of such a curse.

THE RUNE-LORE OF KYLVER:
GOTLAND'S FUÞARK STONE
(From *Rûna*, Vol. I, no. 2, Yule, 1982)

One of the most important, and most argued about, runic inscriptions is that of the fuþark stone of Kylver, Gotland. The stone was first investigated in the year 1902-03. It seems to have been part of a burial chamber, but because of inexact archeological work, its precise original position in uncertain. Apparently, it was a wall or part of the floor of the chamber with the runes facing inward. It seems fairly certain that we are here dealing with a magical formula to hold the dead in the grave or to make the grave more pleasing for him.

Schematically, the inscription appears:

s u e u s

f u þ a r k g w h n i j p ï R s t b e m l ŋ d o

Relevant to our discussion of Sigurd Agrell's Uthark Theory, it is to be noted that the first stave is defective; however, upon personal inspection of the stone some investigators have detected marks indicative of the branches of the fehu rune. The only thing unusual about this fuþark is the apparent reversal of the p- and ï-runes, but this may have had a magical function as we will see.

The other two elements of the inscription, a tree-like form and the fuþark formula sueus are more mysterious. The palindrome is perhaps the Gotlandic form of the word for horse eus (PGmc. e(h)waz) read from "the inside out" (**sue** : **eus** = *eus* : *eus*). This interpretation is also strengthened by the decoding of the tree-symbol at the end of the fuþark. Often the dots or lines which seem to act as mere word dividers or terminals are actually keys to deeper symbolic levels of the formula. 6 + 8 = 14 is contained in the sign (i.e. 6 branches to the left, 8 to the right, their sum being 14). Now, if we apply this to the fuþark and count 6 back from the last rune, and 8 in from the first rune, and also locate the 14th rune in the row we come up with the formula:

ᛖ ᚹ ᛃ
e w ei -or- ewi

This is even an older form of the same word eus: "horse." The use of older forms of the language in magical context, or "archaisizing," is not an uncommon practice in rune-magic, nor is such word-play *eus ~ ewi*—which is also a keystone of the Germanic magico-poetic technique. The form *ewi* is perhaps in an oblique case meaning "to the horse" as a dedication.

This inscription again shows the close relationship between the horse and death-magic and/or curses in the Nordic tradition.

THE UTHARK THEORY AND THE TAROT
(From *Rúna*, Vol. I, No. 2, Yule, 1982)

The Swedish scholar Sigurd Agrell, in a series of learned and inspired works contributed voluminously to the field of runic magic, numerical symbolism, and the cultic aspects of the runic tradition. Many of his researches have probably been discounted because of the framework upon which they were built— his so-called "Uthark-Theory"— which was found by almost all runologists to be unconvincing. However, because those and other ideas of Agrell are so involved with the esoteric aspects or rune-lore, its origins and practices, the Rune-Gild presents this study not only for historical reasons, but also it is hoped, for practical philosophical gain. It is hoped that our fellows can use some of Agrell's ideas (perhaps in modified form) as a starting point for deeper private work as well as inspirational sparks toward expanding the format of our tradition. For those interested in the "Hermetic" traditions, Agrell's works often have refreshing, scientific insight into the genuine ideologies of that school. In this article we want to outline Agrell's still valuable theories concerning the cultic relationship between Mithraism and the runic tradition, his questionable Uthark-Theory, and his ideas concerning the relationship between the Tarot and the runes.

I.

Mithraism is a later development of Zoroastrianism which was being practiced at the time of Roman expansion at the borders of Persia. This religion found a receptive public in the Roman army, where it developed into an all-male warrior religion. These soldiers then brought the faith, along with all its magical features to Europe (where it was syncretized with the Greco-Roman mystery religions). It was these Roman soldiers who built the numerous Mithraic temples to be found along the Rhine, in Britain, etc. According to Agrell, the Germans learned both the alphabet and its magical uses from Mithraic Roman soldiers while the Germans were serving in Roman military units. They then took these practices into Free Germania where it developed into an independent tradition. This process would have taken place sometime around the end of the second century CE.

It would seem that there was indeed some sort of connection, or points of contact, between the Germans along the Rhine and many of those Mediterranean Roman cults of various traditions which had become established all along the western bank of the Rhine and throughout present-day southern Germany and Austria. However, we can only deal with one of these, Mithraism, in this paper. The evidence for a syncretism between Roman Mithraism and the Wôdenic cult is on the one hand circumstantial, i.e. the fact that both cults were principally made up of male warriors (at that time and in that place), that both were initiatory with an emphasis on magical activity, and that both involved homosexual practices; while on the other hand we have some bits of hard evidence as well. One of the most interesting of these comes from the realm of art history. Mithras, in his warrior aspect, is always portrayed riding a chariot armed with bow and spear. In the Mithreum in Dieburg, however, Mithras is seen on horse-back carrying a spear. This has often been interpreted as a clear sign of syncretism with Wôdenism.

II.

Through a complex argument, Agrell builds the theory that the common order of the runes, F-U-Þ-A-R-K, etc., is only a device to conceal the true order which places the "F" at the end of the row, which in turn makes the first rune "U, " the second "Þ", etc. So it is not the fuþark, but the uthark! He attempts to show the relationship between each rune and the cosmology and theology of Mithraism— with varying success (see the table in the Tarot section below).

One of the chief pieces of evidence Agrell uses is the stone of Kylver. In that inscription the first rune, which we suppose to be a ... is defective, and appears as only a vertical stave. This is Agrell's only possible attestation of an Uthark-row, which is really to say that he has no attestations. The fehu-rune of Kylver was probably either damaged or the branches were not very deeply carved. Nevertheless, the brilliant Swede proceeds with his theory.

As he formulated the Uthark, it would appear:

1-u	2-þ	3-a	4-r	5-K	6-g	7-w	8-h
9-n	10-i	11-j	12-ï	13-p	14-z	15-s	16-t
17-b	18-e	19-m	20-l	21-ng	22-d	23-o	24-f

With this formula Agrell set out to apply the theory to the inscriptions themselves— with remarkable results. It seems that when these new numerical values are applied to elder inscriptions many mathematical patterns emerge in the runes which are both consistent, and in harmony with the formulas of Mithraic-Greek gematria. The number 24 plays a dominant role in both, for example— both the fuþark (or uþark!) and the ancient Greek alphabet consisted of 24 signs.

Each fellow may try and apply Agrell's theory to various inscriptions and see the results. One of the more famous runic magical formulaic words is *alu*, which is sometimes seen in scrambled forms, e.g. on the arrow shaft of Nydam. In this formula, Agrell did not see a sensible magical word-formula, but rather a purely numerical one:

$$3 + 20 + 1 + 24$$

This is at once contained all the "Uthark" and indicated *fehu*: "riches." Since this theory was forwarded, an etymology was found, and generally accepted for the word which connected it with "ale," i.e. "ecstasy," and hence to "the magical power which is brought forth in ecstasy."

III.

The possible connection between the runes and the Tarot system has been the subject of speculation throughout the modern runic renaissance. Generally, it was assumed that, if anything, the Tarot was in some way derived from the runic system (since the runes have a documented history over a thousand years older than that of the Tarot). I have usually favored a free correspondence (according to esoteric sense) between the runes and Tarot symbols, rather than the often forced sequential correspondence between the rune-row and the "normal" order of the Trumps (ᚠ = The Magician, etc.). The latter method is the one generally followed in the Armanen-system. Agrell gives us new insight into this process.

Agrell points out the well known fact that the attribution of Hebrew letters to the Tarot Trumps is of relatively late date (late 18th or early 19th century). According to Agrell, the connection between the Tarot and an alphabet occurs in the Greek cultural sphere, not in the Hebrew. This is historically much more convincing, especially since in ancient times it was the Greek alphabet which was most often used in magical manipulations. Even the Hebrew Kabbalah borrowed from its terminology (not to mention its cosmology, etc., etc.)— *ga(m)ma-tria* (G = 3) for example. In late antique times (early in the first millennium of the Common Era) this Greco-Gnostic (Mithraic-Hermetic) magical ideology ruled the Mediterranean world (as its pale third cousin dominates "The Western Magical Tradition" today). The letter-magic practiced in those times was based upon the 24 letter Greek alphabet, but interestingly enough, the general reduction from 24 to 22 letters came not through Hebrew influence but through Roman practice. At that time, the Latin alphabet consisted of 23 letters, but since /y/ could not be found in initial position, it was not used in Roman divination practice which depended on the use of the initial letters of words to form formulaic readings. This Latin 22-letter system then became the underlying one for later magical practice (to which the Hebrew was also added). We can not rule out the possibility that the Tarot symbolism was shaped by either the elder Greek or by a kindred perhaps even Iranian (not necessarily Zoroastrian) system.

The correspondences between the Tarot and the rune-row are then, according to Agrell, indirect ones— both are ultimately derived from the Greco-Mithraic letter-magic system. He then uses the Greek alphabet and its magico-mystical correspondences to explain the Tarot, much in the same way he does to interpret the rune-row. The table presented on the next page is a somewhat modified version of the one printed in *Die pergamenische Zauberscheibe und das Tarockspiel* (pages 97-98). This version re-arranges the order of the *arcana* of the Tarot to agree with the esoteric meanings of the Greek letters— this also makes Agrell's Tarot : runic correspondences more clear. Agrell is of the opinion that the original Tarot order followed the system of Greek letters, but that it became altered when fused with Roman traditions, as outlined above.*

---

* This whole system of the Tarot based on Mithriac symbolism is the subject of a book by Arbaris forthcoming from Rûna-Raven Press entitled *The Magian Tarock*. There too the relationship between the runes and the *arcana* of the Tarot will be further explored.

1. The Fool (*Apis*) — (bull, cow)
2. The Magician (*Bacatus-Typhôn*) — (the demonic)
3. The Priestess (*Cæles-Isis*) — (the divine)
4. The Empress (*Diana*) — (4 elements)
5. The Emperor (*Eon-Aeon*) — (Aion)
6. The Hierophant (*Flamen*) — (Sacrifice and gift)
7. The Lovers (*Gaudium*) — (joy, love)
8. The Chariot (*Hamaxa*) — (crystal-heaven)
9. Justice (*Iustitia*) — (Ananke)
10. The Hermit (*Kronos*) — (Kronos, death)
11. The Wheel of Fortune (*Libera*) — (plants)
12. Strength (*Magnitudo*) — (trees)
13. The Hanged Man (*Noxa*) — (Hekatê)
14. The Star (*Stellae*) — (stars)
15. The Sun (*Victor-Unus*) — (sun)
16. The Devil (*Quirinus*) — (Serapis-Mithras)
17. The Moon (*Trina*) — (feminine)
18. Death (*Orcus*) — (bearer of the dead)
19. The World (*Zodiacus*) — (human)
20. Temperance (*Pluvia*) — (water)
21. Judgement (*Xiphias*) — (Phallus)
22. — (possessions)
23. The Tower (*Ruina*) — (Zeus)
24. — (riches)

IV.

The Uthark-Theory is not held by many today, and this seems only right. Despite the incidence of numerical coincidence between Greek numerological formulas and those of the "Uthark," the fact remains that no artifact or any piece of evidence would indicate that the order was ever anything but that of the fuþark. This Uthark-Theory can not overcome this fact with any of its formulas. The historical arguments are more convincing; however, they too must be modified. It is unlikely that the Mithraic Romans had anything to do with runic origins. The oldest inscriptions date from somewhat before the proposed time of influence, e.g. the spear head of Øvre Stabu ca. 150 CE, and the newly discovered, yet not fully established as runic, inscription on the Meldorf fibula— from the middle of the 1st century CE!

As far as any connection which may be made between the runes and the Tarot through this Mithraic theory, it seems possible that the Tarot was indeed shaped by this, or some related tradition, but the connection of these with rune-lore appears more difficult. Perhaps we could be dealing with some secondary influences on the content of rune-lore after the basic system had been established.

All of this has been intended to stimulate thought — and even meditative activity — because many have experience in both Hermetic systems and in the Tarot, the relationships (mystical or historical) between these traditions can be a field for fruitful work. Although the historical aspect must be kept in logical perspective, this too can be an area of research by fellows of the Rune-Gild.

Part II
Germanic Studies

REINCARNATION IN ÁSATRÚ
(From *The Runestone*, No. 27, Spring, 1979)

Certain modern commentators upon Ásatrú would have us believe that our forefathers held extremely confused ideas concerning the destiny of the human soul after death. This was never the case! Although our forefathers in Ásatrú were never bound by rigid dogma, they had formulated a general ideology based upon direct magico-mystical experience and astute observation of nature— of which they knew themselves to be an integral part. The formula which they developed was rather complex, but no more complex than the multiversal world itself. This complexity baffled the simple-minded monks, and even many later 19th century scholars. It seemed to them that our heathen ancestors only possessed a confused mass of mutually contradictory conceptions— it never occurred to them that all these ideas could have been held at the same time, in a syncretic multiverse.

The "soul" is made up of several entities, each with its own special function. These may be conceived of as "levels of consciousness," or "states of being." Some of these entities which are important to the rebirth process will now be discussed. The *hugr* is the mental faculty, consciousness, seat of the will, etc. The *hamr* is the plastic, image forming material which the *hugr* may use to form new "bodies" for itself— a process much in evidence in the sagas. These concepts are certainly important, but not central to the teaching of reincarnation, or *aptrburðr* (literally translated: "back birth"). Two entities are most involved in this process, the *hamingja* and the *fylgja*. The *hamingja* is a mobile form of magical power, it is the agent by which the *hugr* may create a *hamr*, and it may also be passed from one person to another, either in part or in its entirety. This may constitute either an initiation, or a type of reincarnation respectively. However, it is with the *fylgja* that we enter into the realm of true *aptrburðr*. The *hamingja* is a dynamic force which may be divided and projected for various purposes, but the *fylgja*, or fetch, is attached to the vicinity of its owner for the duration of that individual's life.

Moreover, these various soul-conceptions are considered to have a variety of destinations after death. The *hugr* may go to Valhöll or to Hel, while the *hamr* may remain with the corpse in the burial mound (in certain historical periods) animating the *draugr*, or walking dead. As far as the other two entities are concerned, they may be reborn, within the clanic structure, from generation to generation. The recently dead ancestor would be reborn in the newly born descendents. These diverse beliefs did not come into conflict with one another due to the special way in which the human soul, and the world, were understood. This multiplicity of souls and variety of functions and destinations of these entities after death were concepts which were vigorously attacked by the Christian clergy, and are therefore concepts which must be vigorously pursued and renewed by the folk of Ásatrú, in order that we might again fully know their power.

It must be stressed that, in ancient times, it was not believed that the personal consciousness was reborn, but only certain innate transpersonal powers and abilities— and also certain obligations. The *hamingja-fylgja* complex (these two concepts are often regarded as one during this process) departs from a person's body upon death. In the sagas it is often said that a man who is about to die will be confronted by his *fylgja*. It most often appears as a female being, and furthermore it often has the appearance of a *valkyrja*. (The *valkyrjur* and *fylgjur* seem to be related in many respects.) In any event, once the *fylgja* has departed from the body it may fare with one of the other soul-entities to the barrow, or to either Valhöll or Hel. It may also be passed from a dying man to his son, or beloved kinsman. This latter possibility is especially common with respect to the *ættar—* or *kynfylgja* (clan-fetch) which is usually attached to the head of the clan, and which embodies all the collective power of the clan. However, when the *kynfylgja* (clan-fetch) or *mannsfylgja* (individual's-fetch) takes up abode in one of the other-worlds, it remains there awaiting the birth of the right child to whom it will come and attach itself at the point of *vatni ausa* (sprinkling with water) and *nafn gefa* (name-giving). The *vatni ausa* rite is pre-Christian in origin. These rites are performed by the head of the clan nine days after birth, after the child has shown itself to be worthy of integration into the clan by its physical strength and spiritual power. Both of these rites have a magical intention of aiding the re-integrating process of the *hamingja-fylgja* into the newborn child, and at the same time they serve as ceremonial confirmation of the re-integration which may have taken place over the foregoing nine days of life.

The name which is given to the child is that of a recently dead ancestor. This name is chosen either because the ancestor appeared to the mother, father, or chieftain in a dream during the pregnancy period, or the father, chieftain, or *goði* ascertains the proper name by magical means. The child is then considered to be the ancestor reborn into the clanic structure. That is, the namesake is the bearer of the innate powers, abilities, and obligations of the forebear, but the namesake possesses an original "personality," that is, *hugr*, inspiration (*óðr*), and spirit (*önd*). It is now the task of this new individual, a perfect blend of the powers and obligations of the past and the hopes and responsibilities of the future, to go forth, and by deeds of honor, add to the force of the *hamingja-fylgja*. In this way the "syncretic clan," made up of both the living and the dead, may be viewed as a tree, with the ancestral roots providing the continuing nourishment from the realm of the dead, and the branches providing unending energy from the realm of the living.

This ideology perhaps goes back as far as Indo-European times. Similar beliefs were held by the ancient Greeks, in a form of pre-Pythagorean metempsychosis, and in fact the Pythagorean doctrine was probably for the most part drawn from the indigenous religion, and not "from Egypt," or "from the East." Also, the Thracians and Celts maintained strong rebirth cults. The Rig Vedic Indian culture probably also possessed a doctrine of rebirth similar to that of the other Indo-European cultures.

Old Norse literature is rich in sagas and myths which involve a theme of *aptrburðr*. One of the lesser known, yet most explicit of these is *Þórðar saga hreðu*. In this saga Þórðr goes to battle against a *berserkr* by the name of Bárekr, and during the sword fight, Þórðr is wounded on the arm by Bárekr's poisoned blade. Þórðr returns home and dies. At his funeral feast a son is born to his wife, Helga, and the child is seen to have a scar in the identical place where his father was wounded. The boy was sprinkled with water and given the name Þórðr, after his father. When the boy came into his twelfth winter he set out and avenged his father by killing Bárekr in single combat. It is said, that it seemed to Þórðr that he had grown great by his deed. The mythic hero, Helgi, is reborn in three successive generations, each time bearing the same holy name. Starkaðr (in *Gautreks saga*) is said to be his grandfather, also named Starkaðr, reborn. And of course the greatest of all heros, Sigurðr Fáfnisbani, is most certainly the rebirth of his father, Sigmundr. (Another, perhaps more ancient mode of naming involved the variation of a portion of the name.) Ragnarök provides us with extremely important examples of *aptrburðr*. Along with the other Gods who are reborn, or live past the dissolution of the world, there are two figures known as the Gods of Vengeance— Víðarr and Váli. Víðarr avenges the death of his father, Óðinn, while Váli avenges the death of Baldr. These two Gods of Vengeance may be considered to be *aptrburðir* of Óðinn and Baldr respectively. However, this constitutes one of the greatest mysteries (*rúnar*) of Ásatrú, and is much to complex to fully discuss here— but the relevant texts in both *Eddas* can become fruit-bearing branches for religious meditation.

Two elements played important roles in the heathen ideology of *aptrburðr*, 1) ritual action: the *vatni ausa*— naming rite, and 2) the responsibilities of the "reborn" to the "dead" to perform deeds of honor, and to avenge their deaths if necessary. The verb "to avenge" in Old Norse is "*hefna*." This word actually contains the root meaning: "to release," that is, to release the soul(s) of the dead in order that they might proceed to their proper destinations already mentioned above. This includes the release of the— *hamingja-fylgja* so that it/they may more completely be reborn within the clan. A third important element which aids in this interlace between the worlds of the dead and the living is made up of various initiatory rites, which have a transmission of power or wisdom from the realm of the dead to that of the living as their principles function— thereby more completely integrating the two into a syncretic one.

Now, it must be said that these beliefs are still viable today! These answers to age-old questions are based upon millennia of observation of, and experience in, the natural order of the multiverse by our own forebears— and not the "answers" foisted upon us by unnatural and unwholesome monks. We may still follow the ways of our forefathers by, 1) naming our children right, in accordance with both the ancient naming ritual and customs of name choosing, and 2) fulfilling all our responsibilities to our ancestors.

* * * * * * *

Vatni Ausa Ceremony

1) The Mother lays the child in the lap of the Father (or the head of the clan, or *goði*). The terms "Mother" and "Father" may be understood symbolically here.

2) The Father sprinkles pure spring water upon the child using either a ladle, or a spring of evergreen, saying:

"*Ek verp vatni þetta barn á, ok gef honum nafnit*
_____(name) (*eptir afa/ömmu sínum/sinni.*)"

(English translation: "I throw water on this child and
give it the name _____ (after its grandfather/
grandmother) (or some other ancestor).

This may be incorporated into other *blótar*, but in any case it should be a joyous occasion— for the forefathers are again among us!

"FATE" IN ÁSATRÚ
(From *The Runestone*, No. 31, Spring, 1980)

In reading about Germanic mythology and religion, how often have we Ásatrúarfólk come across statements concerning the "fatalism" of the heroes, or of the religious world-view of the ancient Norse in general? Many times, no doubt. But just what did "fate" mean to the Ásatrúarfólk of old? There have grown up many misconceptions surrounding this word and concept, so central to our faith. An analysis of this idea from the perspective of Ásatrú may shed considerable light on this sacred subject.

In English, the word "fate" is loaded with a semantic quality of predestination, i.e., a transcendental force has already pre-determined that such and such will happen to a person, folk, etc. The two Germanic words most often translated by "fate" are the Old Norse *ørlög* and the Old English *wyrd*. A close study of these two words is quite revealing. *Ørlög* is a compound of the prefix *ør-*: "a primal, oldest, outermost, etc.", and the root *lög*, which is a plural construction meaning "law(s)" but originally, and literally "layers." *Ørlög* is the primal-law, or primal-layers which a person "lays down" by his or her past action. This is also true of cosmic processes, but that is another saga. The word *wyrd* contains a similar quality. *Wyrd* is a feminine noun developed from the past tense of the Old English word *weorðan*: "to become," or more basically "to turn." Thus, *wyrd* is that which has become (those layers already laid) which affect the present and the future. In Old Norse this word is *urðr*, the name of the first Norn, similarly developed from the Old Norse verb *verða*, "to become." .

This is the metaphysic behind the Germanic system of law, such as English Common Law, based upon precedent (past layers of action) which determine what should be done present and future. This is in sharp contrast to the Judeo-Roman form of law based upon decree from a transcendental source (e.g. god or king)— a situation in which we increasingly find ourselves today.

So far it is obvious that the Germanic concept of "fate" is closely connected with concepts of time and causality. That which has become (the past) conditions the present and the future. This, as so much else in Ásatrú, is a common sense approach to the matter. The mystery of the Three Norns provides further keys to the understanding of wyrd. The names of the Norns are Urðr (wyrd), Verðandi ("that which is becoming," from the same root as *urðr*) and Skuld ("that which should/must [become]"). The first two condition, but do not determine the third. These conditions are produced by the deeds of the person who receives the fruits of those deeds. The Norns are not causal agents but rather the numinous organisms through which the energies of actions are received, transformed, and re-directed back to their source.

Within the psychosomatic (i.e. soul/body) complex of the individual this functions through the *fylgja*, or "fetch." This psychic organism, which is attached to an individual, and receives the energies of individual and environmental actions, formulates them into a reprojectable form and then projects them back into the life of the individual where they have their effect. This is a totally amoral process, and purely organic in structure. This *fylgja* is passed from one life to the next along family lines, or sometimes it is transferred free from clanic limitations, thus, in either case, passing the accumulated past action (*ørlög*) from one life to another. It seems clear that the old Germanic concept of "fate" is in no way similar to the Christian concept of predestination, but rather quite akin to the Sanskrit concept of karma, a term which has also suffered at the hands of Christian misinterpretation. The ancient Ásatrúarfólk knew that they shaped their own destinies as a result of their own past actions.

It is a heroic virtue to struggle against *ørlög*, always knowing that the greatness of its power will overcome the force of the personal will. There is, however, another path— that of the *vitki* (the "wise one, magician"). Many great heroes, such as Sigurðr and Starkaðr, are also vitkar. A *vitki* is one who first knows his or her *ørlög*, and then intentionally and willfully chooses to follow it, or in rare cases to alter it through magical means. Often the *vitki* will investigate *ørlög* to find out how better to follow its inner guidance.

The *vitki*-hero may investigate *ørlög* in three realms of past action, 1) personal, 2) clanic, and 3) metapersonal. The first is past action contained within the perimeters of the present life time, while the latter two may be roughly considered as "past lives," one genealogically determined and the other extra-clanic. The first realm can be investigated through personal retrospective of past deeds in one's life. The clanic realm is investigated through genealogical history, which in olden times was an important type of numinous knowledge. The metapersonal, which is drawn from the collective unconscious, and which probably should not be understood as a "reincarnation" of the individuality, may be undertaken under self-guidance, or with the aid of fellow Ásatrúarfólk— this technique is rampant among the storefront occultists, and is often dressed in the most shoddy of cosmologies. A similar technique may also be used for genealogical research. In all these forms of wyrd investigation, the practice of runic divination can become an invaluable aid.

The concept of *ørlög*, and the knowledge of it, played a central role in the religious world of the ancient Germanic tribesman, and it should again occupy an important place in the hearts of modern Ásatrúarfólk. *Ørlög* must, however, be approached in the old way of the North, free from the Judeo-Christian concepts of predestination and transcendental fatalism. The Ásatrúarfólk are not manipulated by "fate", but rather are responsible for their own *ørlög*!

THE SUMBLE
(From *Raven Banner* 26, Winter 1979)

No other early essay of mine had more widespread influence than this one. It sprang from listening to a lecture given by Paul Bauschatz at the University of Texas in 1976. From there, through this article, and from practical experiments in the Austin Kindred with Mitchell Edwin Wade, the practice of the Sumble has spread far and wide. [Edred]

Often the venerable Germanic ritual feast has been profanely described as a drunken brawl. To be sure there were plenty of those— but the sacred ritual feast is sometimes ignored in such discussions, perhaps because some writers fear what they may find there. These feasts presuppose a cosmos in which humans and gods are at one before forces influencing them both, all three of these elements being parts of an organic whole.

The rite of feasting was known throughout the ancient Germanic territories. In Old Norse it was called *sumbl*, in Old High German *sumbal*, and in Old English *symbel*. The word may be a compound of *sum-*, "coming together," and *-öl*, "ale;" that is, "a gathering of the imbibing of inspiring drink." The structure of this rite is simple and beautiful. The participants gather, and the host sits them in a particular order within the hall (according to their relationship to the host). The wife, husband, and so on, of the host bears forth the drinking horn or cup and gives it to the host. The host drinks and invokes the god(s) and/or goddess(es) to the sumble by reciting a *full*. (A *full* is a formal speech of invocation spoken in ritualized drinking.) The cupbearer presents the drink to each of the guests in turn. Each participant speaks a *full*, boast or oath before drinking. A short narrative tale or part of such a tale may be interwoven into the body of the speech. A *skald* or *scôp* may also sing a heroic narrative between the speeches of the guests. After each participant speaks her or she may present or be presented with a gift. The sumble never "degenerates" into a drunken brawl. The cup may pass around the hall only once, or several times, as has been predetermined. Also, no solid food is ingested at a sumble— only intoxicating drink (mead, ale or beer). The rite is ended by a formal declaration by the host.

The best literary examples of the sumble are to be found in the first half of *Bêowulf*, and in the "Lokasenna" and the "Hymiskvíða" of the *Poetic Edda*. In these examples it is shown that the gods too take part in this type of feasting.

Now to an esoteric interpretation of the events of the sumble. Sitting within a hall in a particular arrangement signifies the "many-ness" of the world ordered within the whole— the hall. The intoxicating drink is filled with numinous inspiration which is the gift of the gods. This drink symbolizes the continuous organic power which envelops both humans and gods. With the speeches the speakers shape this force in an aesthetic fashion and in a way that is beneficial to the community and to him/herself. The narrative material which is interwoven into the *full* or oath is drawn from the past actions of the heroes of one's own people. A heroic event is thus linked to the present, leading into a non-past/present construct (= "the future"). The gift is an exchange which is an outward and lasting symbol of the inner event of the speech. The singing of the *skald* or *scôp* symbolizes the continuous flow of past and present into one another in the sumble. All in all, the sumble is a ritual enactment of the holiness ("wholly-ness") of the multiverse and humankind's active place in it.

In the sumble, past and present consciously flow together in a spiritual center, where humans and gods become one and where they ritually act together in order to shape that which is to come, in accordance with holy principles.

ANCIENT FOUNDATIONS OF THE RUNE-CULT IN EUROPE
(From *The Runestone*, No. 36, Summer, 1981)

A cultus involving secret lore and initiatory mysteries existed in the North since Neolithic times. Through the centuries a system of elaborate graphic symbology was also developed in conjunction with the cultus. However, the exact symbolic content and use of these signs must forever remain clouded behind the deep mists of time. But we can say with no little conviction that these were the nights in which the cult of the mysteries — the gild of the runes — began to take shape. The glyphs were eventually systematized and used by members of a virtually pan-Germanic traditional network of "wise ones." Much of the content of these traditions stemmed directly from the Indo-European traditions, as tempered by local indigenous populations.

Perhaps a historical digression is in order here. It must be clear what is meant by "Indo-European," "Germanic," and "indigenous populations." From the time of the recession of the ice sheets (between ca. 10,000 and 7,000 BCE) in the twilight of the Ice Age, the region of what is now northern Germany, Denmark, and southern Norway and Sweden was populated with tribes belonging to the great Old European Culture. This Old European Culture, which has its reflections on a global scale as the Megalith Culture, was generally characterized by an agricultural economy based upon large sedentary aggregates of population, an egalitarian political system, with matrilineal (but not necessarily matriarchal) traditions, and a Goddess-centered religion. These cultures seem to have been peace-loving, since no weapons are found in their graves. In the third millennium BCE the region began being invaded by a warlike people from the east and south-east. These were the Indo-European speaking, horse breeding warriors who were to fundamentally and forever re-shape the region. These people had a highly mobile, horse-dominated, pastoral, semi-nomadic culture. They would settle for a short period, building semi-subterranean houses, and burying their dead in mounds; but then move on into new territory— or at least send out expeditions into new lands. Their political structure was a simple and highly flexible hierarchical aristocracy. They were patriarchal and patrilineal. War was their greatest obvious skill; however, they had developed methods of infiltration into, and assimilation of indigenous populations which were very effective. It seems that their normal invasion pattern involved a spear-head of young warriors led by experienced war-lords, who would establish themselves as minority rulers in neighboring foreign territories. This would often involve them in war but the locals were rarely a match for horse drawn war chariots. But their aim was not the destruction of the indigenous group, but rather their assimilation. Indo-European cultural features (i.e., language, religion, political and clanic structure, and technology) became the superstructure of the new synthetic culture; however, a great deal of the indigenous people's values, lore and ways were incorporated— especially when the culture had once and for all become sedentary. In the region of northern Germany and southern Scandinavia this Indo-European/Old European synthesis gave rise to what is called "Germanic Culture."

The myth of the first war between the Æsir and the Vanir, and its peaceful solution in ultimate assimilation under the hegemony of the Æsir (we never hear anything about the Vanir who were not taken into the

Æsir camp as hostages). This pattern is a usual one for the Indo-European peoples when they came into contact with native populations, in Europe, that is. Another example of this is the historicized myth of the Rape of the Sabine Women by the Romans recorded by Livy.

But what has this got to do with runes? In the first place, there is nothing which does not have to do with runes, but more specifically, the rich graphic symbolism (especially found in rock-carvings) and the cultic dynamism found in the period during and immediately after this cultural assimilation indeed seems to be the age in which the foundations of the runic cult were laid.

In the Germanic Bronze Age (ca. 1500 - 500 BCE), the northern tribes began to flourish in their now already ancient homeland. Linguistically, these tribes were still virtually monolingual (a language called Early Proto-Germanic by linguists), with any existing dialects readily mutually intelligible. The religious symbology was probably also closely related, and of course continued to be so throughout the paleo-pagan period. Bronze Age rock-carvings found mainly in Sweden and Norway already show a spear-god (Óðinn), a hammer-god (Þórr), a ski-god (Ullr), etc. Besides a mythic material, largely inherited from Indo-European archetypes, there also developed a unique Germanic system of holy signs. The degree to which these signs (sometimes called pre-runic) were actually systematized at that time is difficult to tell since they do seem to belong to a single formal tradition, and given the remarkable cultural unity (religious as well as linguistic), it would seem highly probable that the signs represent an esoteric, magical system of signs used by clan members trained in the traditional secrets as a means to communicate the depths of the secrets to one another and between humanity and the gods. There is nothing unusual in this, or in the fact that it was an inter-tribal tradition— similar patterns are found in Asia and Africa.

Without going into too many details in this format, it can be said that long before the advent of the rune-stave systems as outlined in No. 35 of *The Runestone* in the article entitled "The Fuþark," there was a well developed network of intra-Germanic tradition which preserved esoteric lore in some systematic way. Without the entry of the rune-staves and the concept of writing into the system, this most ancient "Pre-runic system" would have remained almost invisible. But as the staves came into use, beginning in the 2nd century CE, a pattern began to emerge.

This event was much like the infusion of a dye into organic tissue— elaborate, previously hidden patterns emerge and are recorded forever. The level of complexity inherent in the runic system, and the level of continuity and integrity maintained by it over the centuries make this possible. We can trace much of the work of this gild of runemasters because we at least have a fraction of the physical results of their work— the runic inscriptions. Therefore, technical aspects of their religious symbolism and magical import may be studied— although this requires extensive training.

On the other hand, the nature of the gild itself and its organization remained almost totally hidden— or has been fancifully reconstructed on the model of modern occult schools! What is clear is that the runes and their lore constituted a vast system which had to be learned and therefore also taught— taught by a **master** (i.e., one skilled in the art) and learned by an apprentice (i.e., one with the will and ability to learn the art). This teaching and learning process is of course the pattern seen later in all medieval guild systems. However, it must be remembered that the gild was originally an Ásatrú sacrificial association. That is, it had a sacred purpose. The religio-magical gild was then the model for the later developing craft guilds. The medieval free masons were an example of this type of guild.

These archaic gilds did not have centers of teaching or universities (which were originally also organized like guilds) nor did they maintain a complex initiatory system of "grades," etc. None of this would have been practical in the clano-centric social structure of the Germanic peoples in the Bronze and Iron Ages, and continuing through the Viking Age. The ancient rune-gild was indeed a phantomic, and hidden "order" in more than one way. It was maintained by two types of institutions in which its masters participated, 1) the local clanic wise one(s), to whom the younger members eager after the secrets of the world could go for instruction, and 2) the wandering wise ones, who not only as magicians, but also as poets, singers of songs, and tellers of tales easily got free passage between tribal groups. These two types, and a true master would have to be both at one time or another, mutually supported one another in an organic system which was at once conservative, dynamic, and open to new concepts— once they were re-shaped along the lines of the tradition.

This then was the general shape of the ancient rune-gild by the late Roman and early Migration Ages (ca. 150-400 CE). This formulation, as well as each of its further evolutionary stages, has much to teach us in our re-formulation of the work today. We must both be able to skillfully ascertain what the actual historical nature of the ancient forms were, and at the same time maintain the spirit and skills of adaptation to new situations which lie at the heart of the Germanic genius.

I, THE RUNE MASTER
(From *The Runestone*, No. 38, Winter, 1981)

In this article we will look at a runic formula which tells us something of the psychological realm of the old Germanic runemaster— and try to learn what this can mean to our conceptions today.

The formulaic use of the first person singular pronoun **ek**: "I," followed by either a seemingly official title or initiatory or "magical" name is quite common in the elder runic corpus. It occurs a total of at least twenty-one times in extant inscriptions dating from between 200 and 600 CE This **ek** plus noun/nominal adjective formula is found only in the North and seems firmly entrenched in the cultic organization which supported the old runic tradition in Scandinavia.

One particular formula **ek erilaR** (e.g. on the stone of Järsberg), which occurs eight times in the elder corpus, is at once informative, yet problematic. In the first place, from a linguistic point of view, we can not be absolutely sure what the significance of the term **erilaR** might have been. It has been suggested (e.g. by Jacobsen and Moltke *Danmarks Runeindskrifter* [1941]) that the term was originally the tribal name (H)eruli. However, it seems rather more likely that it was some term for a great and powerful man which in this case became specialized in the runic realm as "runemaster." Otherwise, the word developed in a more general sense as Old English *eorl*: "warrior" —> "earl," and in Old Norse *jarl* —> "noble man." If the derivation is from the tribal name Heruli, then this would seem to be because this tribe (which had its original homeland in the Danish islands) was well-known for its experts in runic practice. The Heruli were subsequently pushed out of their home by invading Danes from Skåne and scattered themselves throughout Europe in the Age of Germanic Migrations. In any event, the final result as far as **erilaR** is concerned is the same. It has the semantic force of "one skilled in rune-knowledge"— which was probably a general title for a master of the runic art.

Another informative type is that which incorporates a descriptive title (or adjective) into the formula, often alone, but sometimes alongside **erilaR** or another seemingly more official title. Since erilaR has been discussed exhaustively elsewhere, we will concentrate on some examples of this type which may well illustrate the point of this article. There are thirteen examples of this kind of formula which have thus far been found among the runic inscriptions. We do not have space to treat all of them, however; a few typical examples will demonstrate the principle at work.

The oldest of all these inscriptions (from ca. 200 CE) is the brooch of Gårdlösa which reads: **ekunwodiR**, and which literally translated would mean: "I, the un-raging one," i.e., the runemaster designated by the **ek** formula is, for purposes of this magical work, going by a name which emphasizes the quality of calmness and freedom from agitation with which he wants to load the brooch and hence the owner of the brooch for whom he is working. A similar formula is found on the fragmentary stone of Nordhuglo, which reads:

ekgudijaungandiRih/ / /

"I, the priest (*gudja* —> *goði*), (am) the un-enchanted one (i.e., the one not open to [evil] magical influences)." The last two staves begin a word, or are part of a formula which is broken off. Here the runic *goði* is identifying himself with the quality **ungandiR**, and attaching this banishing power to the stone and ultimately to the grave-mound to which the stone was originally attached.

Some other characterizing names with which the runemaster identifies himself for magical effect are: **wiwaR**, "the sanctifier;" **wiwila**, "the little sanctifier" (perhaps the apprentice of a **wiwaR**); **þirbijaR**, "the sleep-maker;" **wakraR**, "the wakeful one." There are further examples with the formulaic **ek**, as well as in isolation where the *ek* might be understood.

But what does all this tell us about the psychological world of the ancient Germanic runemaster, and what can these stones and pieces of metal teach us today? In the first place it tells us that the ego (the word is after all merely the Latin first person singular pronoun cognate to **ek**) plays an important role in the conceptual world of the runemaster. His way was not to negate the ego, but rather to develop and ennoble it— ultimately through identification with divine or archetypal qualities. He boldly proclaimed himself at the beginning of these formulas— it was with his personal power (i.e. forces over which his own will had control) that he loaded the objects for magical purposes. This fact accounts for the sometimes seemingly strange formulas which instead of directly saying "keep evil magic away from this place," will use a personalized magical formula such as: **ek gudija ungandiR**. From what we know about the Germanic spiritual world, this does not represent empty boasting or "crass egoism," but is rather a phenomenon of conscious fulfillment of duty and responsibility. The **erilaR** won his position through hard work within his community and under the training of some runic teacher and was bound to serve the community and to carry on the tradition.

Another important aspect of these inscriptions is the fact that rarely does the name in question appear to be a regular or common proper name, but tends to be a special title or characterizing magical name which was probably coined for the occasion of the inscription— or drawn from a storehouse of evocatory names available to the runemaster. With the help of these runic formulas the erilaR could evoke these magical roles or personas, identify himself with them through the **ek** = magical power formula, subsequently bring them under the control of his will, and direct them in the desired manner. Thus the formula in question represents a transformational process for the runemaster.

This psychological dynamic is a powerful one with which we can identify today— and one which is fundamentally in accordance with the whole of the Germanic world view. The way of the **erilaR** does not teach that humanity is the tool of "higher" forces, nor that the unschooled brute-will of man can have its way— but rather that the self, working in tandem with the archetypal forces and trained in the runic traditions, can bring the will of man into harmony with world order— and thus make it a most effective and powerful essence in the cosmos.

HIDDEN GOD-LORE
Are the Gods Our Ancestors?
(From *Rúna*, vol. I, no. 1, Midsummer, 1984)

The writer of a recent piece of rather angrily worded correspondence inquired whether or not we of the Rune-Gild "believed" that the gods were our ancestors. (If so the correspondent wished to inform us that he wanted nothing to do with us!) Apparently, although the somewhat non-verbal nature of the letter leaves us some room for speculation, the writer holds one side of a continuum of positions on the nature of the gods commonly held among those calling themselves Germanic heathens. He apparently wants to see the gods as purely "spiritual," anthropomorphic beings who transcend the world of man— Midgard. The other extreme, is that of euhemerism. This holds that the gods were indeed mortal men in days of yore, but men who possessed magical powers and who to some extent passed these powers on to their descendants. From the standpoint of Odianism neither position is entirely true— but both reflect certain truths.

To a large extent this conclusion is attainable through thoughtful analysis of the (mainly Odinic) tradition and history of the folk. As far as the categorical rejection of the idea that the "gods are our ancestors;" anyone who does this rejects a whole body of genuine Germanic tradition from the English, Norse and Goths. I will offer but one accessible example from each. The English kings knew themselves to be the scion of Wôden. Many of the Old Norse *fornaldarsögur* ("sagas of olden times") were actually prefaces to historical sagas and were used to make a panegyric genealogical link between a historical king and a god— usually Óðinn or Freyr. The greatest example of this is that of the *Völsunga saga*, the first sentence of which reads: "Here begins the saga, and it tells of a man who was named Sigi and called by men the son of Óðinn." This is the beginning of the genealogy of Sigurðr Fáfnisbani the ultimate hero of the Germanic peoples. According to this elaborate saga genealogy, this line of descent links the Norwegian king Hákon Hákonarson (1217-63) with Sigurðr— and to the primal Al-faðir-Óðinn. According to Jordanes (*Getica* XII, 78) the Goths called their ancestors *Ansis* (PGmc. *ansiuz*: "sovereign divinities") who are further described as *semideos* (Latin) "half-gods." But here, as in the other examples, the pattern is clear, since these Ansis are considered to be the ancestors only of the *proceres*— the chieftains.

This last point must be kept in mind from a rune-Odinic viewpoint. The ancestral "blood" of the gods only flows through the æthelings— through the noble ones. In any event, the traditions of the ancients show clearly that at least some of our folk — the æthelings of Óðinn — are descended from him in some quasi-genetic way. That is, our connection to Óðinn is not primarily or merely "contractual," but "genetic." He did not "choose" us— he **is within** us.

But does this mean that at one point Óðinn was a man and begat children on human women? The tradition seems to point in another— more mytho-magical direction. The "fatherhood" of Óðinn always has some magic connected to it, and exists on a mythic level. It is a metaphor for the "Gift of Óðinn" — consciousness — which makes man what he is. (See "Völuspá" 17-18.) Óðinn and all the gods remain always gods (although they may sometimes appear in human or semi-human shape in man's perception).

Ultimately, the truths that must be borne in mind by those who know themselves to be æthelings are: the gods are forever gods and were never men (Óðinn lives as much today as he did in days of yore), and the link between god and ætheling is one of "kinship" (similarity) first— not one of "contract." The implications of this are astounding. It is because of this empathetic or metaphorically "genetic" link that direct knowledge of Óðinn is possible— and that æthelings may know one another as brothers and sisters. The original Gift of Óðinn was given to a "primordial ancestor"— who has passed it on to his ætheling scion. This is the first, last and only forthcoming true "gift" of Óðinn— all else must be won by means of this holy weapon. Simply put: Óðinn is our ancestor in a mythic sense in that his divine pattern provides for human consciousness and intelligence, and so forth; but since he was never a fleshly man he can not have been an ancestor in the profane sense.

Heill Óðinn!

EUHEMERISM IN ÁSATRÚ
(From *The Runestone*, No. 53 (Fall, 1985))

From the esoteric standpoint, and from the general scholarly view as well, the idea of Euhemerism— the notion that Óðinn was a historical human being deified by his followers and descendants is impotent and unlikely. The whole concept is one that spiritually weakens the position of Ásatrú and exposes our theology to ridicule in many scholarly circles.

Our Indo-European ancestors were highly capable of abstract thought— and of abstract theology. The name *Wôð-an-az ("master of inspired mental activity") is essentially a deification of a psychic concept— *wôð- (Old Norse óðr). In a theological sense, to reduce this elegant abstract, which reflects a level of intellectual superiority over many other theologies, to a historical level seems unwise.

In the history of religion, Euhemerism is invoked when those hearing the tales of the Gods are either no longer impressed with, or believe in, the objective numinous reality of the Gods (as was the case with Euhemerus himself in 4th century BCE Greece) or when there is an actual effort to denigrate the Gods (as with the monk Saxo Grammaticus). Saxo wanted to show an evolutionary trend based on classical models in which the giants were overcome by the Ases— human magicians who could dupe the giants— who were in turn overcome by Christians. We will not consider Saxo's methods or motivations here. Historically, Euhemerism seems to be the humanizing of the numinous in periods when man has lost, or is losing, access to the spiritual realms.

The most often quoted author with regard to Norse Euhemerism is Snorri— usually extracted from the "Prologue" to the *Edda*. See also his introductory chapters in the *Ynglinga saga*. In it we read that the Æsir are actually Trojans who escaped the fall of Troy (see Homer's *Iliad*) and who came North from their Trojan homeland in Asia Minor. This "Trojan Saga" was a standard, virtually obligatory convention for medieval writers. It is a tradition that stems from the Romans' desire to connect themselves more firmly with the Greek national epics of Homer. This was done by Virgil in the *Aeneid* (which was the most widely read text, besides the Bible, in the ancient and medieval world). Paris was founded by the Trojans, etc. All of this was part of a convention whereby one national group could gain prestige by attaching itself to this international tradition— the Romans from the Greeks, and from the Romans to the rest of Europe as Christianity progressed.

It is beyond most reasonable doubt that Snorri is following general medieval convention in his "Prologue" to the *Edda* and elsewhere. The "Prologue" seems to be an inorganic appendage to the work as a whole— a sort of obligatory medieval explanation of the origin of the Æsir. Certainly, nowhere in the *Elder Edda* or in any fragment of pre-Christian poetry do we find any evidence for the "Trojan Saga" of the Æsir. In short, the "historical" evidence for Óðinn as magician/chieftain rests on a Christian/medieval tradition which runs counter to that of the pre-Christian age.

Was Óðinn ever a man? The theological approach to the recent articles has been to declare that Óðinn was both a God and a man (where have we heard this before?). This seems like an intriguing solution, and there is a fair amount of hard evidence that points in this direction. But it is substantially different than one might at first expect. The problem with the question: "Was Óðinn ever a man?" is with the verb. Óðinn was not; Óðinn is. The second problem is with the number: a man. This puts Óðinn, or some essential and unique aspect of him, into an isolated historical position. Once a God has become a man and that man dies, the relevance of that God is apt to recede into an almost infinitesimal historical category. The God becomes a prisoner of his unique manifestation.

It would be more meaningful to ask if men are ever Óðinn? The historical answer to this is yes, men have been Óðinn in the past. As most Odians know, the High One is called by many names. Each name expresses an aspect or function of the God. In the runic corpus we see several examples of the runemasters taking on magical / functional personas that are very similar or identical to those expressed by Odinic epithets or Óðinsheiti. When, for example, we read on the 6th century Järsberg stone from central Sweden: *Ubaz haite, Hrabanaz haite* . . . (The Malicious-One I am called, Raven I am called...) we are very much reminded of the "Grímnismál" (st. 47 and following) which give a catalog of Odinic names and which begin: *Hétomk Grímnir, hétomk Gangleri* ... (I am called the Masked-One, I am called the Way-Weary-One...). Here we see the very archaic practice of a shamanistic assumption of a god-form by the rune-master. The functional forms he assumes correspond to the willed direction of his operation. This was a practice carried out by the members of an entire inter-tribal network of runesters over a period of several centuries. Óðinn may never have been a man, but men have become Óðinn many times— and can do so again.

The main problem with Euhemerism seems to be the tendency to reduce the timeless God (or some essential aspect of him) to a unique, isolated historical form. Therefore, once this momentary aspect is gone— we have lost something essential about the God. In some ways Euhemerism is almost the "Jesusizing" of Óðinn. In any event, what do we, as Odinians, gain by a historical, humanized Óðinn? Nothing, as far as I can see— he is dead: "Of what gain is a good man dead?" ("Hávamál" 71). It seems wisest to keep the Gods as timeless living entities— as present today as they were yesterday if we will but open our eyes.

THE HOLY
(From *Rúna*, Vol. I., No. 2, Yule, 1982)

I

Many of the grand and elegant conceptions of our folk went by the wayside in the wake of the church sponsored corrosion of our spiritual and intellectual hoard. One of the most powerful of these is the idea of "the holy," and more particularly of its two-sided nature. Here, we would like to outline this concept, which although it is one of the inherited elements from our Indo-European heritage, finds a special Germanic form which can tell us much of the nature of the holy, things holy, and the place of these in the lives of humanity. This posits a basic religio-magical question, and it is one to which a highly satisfactory and transforming answer is possible. Once the runester is able to conceive of the holy in the way outlined below, he or she will be well on the way to ridding him or herself of the false Judeo-Christian idea which has attempted to destroy our idea of the holy. Most may have already conceived of the world in this way, but it is hoped that the following essay will, in any case, be able to give more shape and definition to this basic cosmological mystery (*heimsrún*).

The holy is a whole but double-sided concept. This formula does not need to rely on theory only, for we know that our ancestors had, until the coming of Christianity, two distinct words to express this dichotomy. However, some Germanic languages lost one of the roots, while others only preserved one in limited contexts, and the clear articulation was lost in a dark haze. In Proto-Germanic, these words were *wîhaz and *hailagaz, in Old English wîh and hâlig, in Old High German wîh and heilig, in Gothic weihs and hailags, in Old Norse vé and heilagr. As can be seen, we only now perceive the latter half of the pair, in the word "holy." The wîh half has disappeared— but with the return of this concept to our consciousness the road to the runes is greatly eased.

II

The etymologies of the two words show the first step in understanding this complex.

Proto-Germanic *wîhaz developed from Proto-Indo-European *vîk: "to separate," and important cognates in other Indo-European languages are: Sanskrit *vinákti*: "sorted, sifted" and Latin *vic-tima*: "sacrificial animal."

Therefore, something which is *wîhaz* is separate in some way from the every-day, it is "completely other." To this concept, Rudolf Otto gave the name *numinosum tremendum*, or the terrifying power, or numen.

PGmc. *hailagaz comes from a PIE root *kail-: "to be whole, invulnerable" and it has a wide range of IE cognates which reflects the range of meaning in Germanic itself, e.g. Middle Welsh *coel*: "omen," Old Irish *cél*: "augury," Balto-Slavic *kailústikan-*: "health," Old Church Slavonic *cél*: "whole, healthy." This concept is given the name *numinosum fascinosum*— the fascinating, attractive power, or numen. That which keeps things whole and healthy.

As we explore the meanings of these concepts more deeply, their distinctions and interdependence will become more evident.

III
*Wîhaz

The basic root *wîh- is found in a telling distribution of meanings in the Germanic dialects. As a noun, it can be used as:

1. "a site for cultic activity, sacred ground"— ON vé,
OHG wîh, OE wîh
2. "a grave mound" ON vé:(in the runic inscriptions of Glavensdrup, Vedelspang, Gottorp, and Vordingborg.
3. "a site where court is held"—ON vé-bönd (ropes used to mark boundaries of the court-stead)
4. "an idol, or divine image"— OE wêoh
5. "a standard or flag"— ON vé

Further, it is seen as a name for the divine forces themselves. Of course the most famous of these is the third "brother" of Óðinn in the divine trial Óðinn-Vili-Vé (cf. *Runelore*). But also in ON we see the plural term veár for "the gods" in general. In a compound form, one of the most famous of all runic inscriptions, the Nordendorf fibula II (Frankish? ca. 600 CE), preserves the name *Wîgi-þonar*: "the sanctifying Þórr." (It must, however, be mentioned that this *wigi-* could also mean "battle," from an entirely different root *wig-*. This would normally fit better with the original warrior function of Þunaraz.) But there is good evidence to show that Þórr became a "sanctifying god" in the late pagan forms of paleopagan Ásatrú— under the influence of functional syncretisms with the lore of the Christian church.

Wîh- is also used in a verb form, ON *vîgja*: "to consecrate." This originally would have meant "to set apart in numinous power," and thereby "to load with numinous power." In the magico-formulaic language of runic inscriptions the term *vîgja* is again connected with Þórr in the younger periods— e.g. examples of þur uiki (þasi runaR): "Þórr consecrate these runes!" or similar formulas. In the elder period we have, besides Nordendorf II mentioned above, three other attestations of *wîh-. The oldest (ca. 200 CE) of these is probably connected with Wôðanaz— the bucket of Vimose. It may be translated: "A(nsuR)! I, Asula ('the little AnsuR') sanctify Andag to **the** AnsuR ('Wôden')." Another attestation on the spear shaft of Kraghul (500-550) reminds us of the other worldly, often "deadly" aspects of the word: the inscription, according to Wolfgang Krause, reads in part: wî(h)ju g[aiRa]— "I consecrate to the spear"— i.e. "mark for sacrificial death." This idea has had a long life, and we see an example of it in the Middle Ages (in Canterbury) in a talisman against sickness which can be translated: "Giril, bringer of sickness, fare thou now away, thou art found out! Þórr consecrates (**uigi**—read: "kills") thee, lord of the Thurses!" The third elder attestation is discussed below.

Originally, *wîh indicated the *numinosum tremendum* and the state of that realm in which it dwells— that "quite otherly" (cf. ON *véar*. "the gods," and *vé*). This led to the natural identification of *wîh- with locations of the phenomenon which were enclosed and set apart because of their sacred nature (cf. ON vé, OHG wîh, OE wîh ON vébönd). Also, objects in which the *wîh- had been concentrated became identified with it (cf. OE wêoh, and ON vé: "a standard or flag"). The verb *wîhian* indicated the action by which things could be "sacrilized," and given to that other realm. This could be accomplished by a variety of actions, e.g. sacrificing the object, bringing it into contact with the location of the wîh, identifying the object with the wîh by means of symbols, etc. Once in this state the object was protected as a sacred thing (hence the protection formula: Þórr vîgi . . .). The bridging of the gap between the world of *wîh- and the mundane world is the true purpose of re-ligion— when this is accomplished, a state of awe (ON œgi-) comes over the subject. This bridge, this Bifröst, exists within all humanity all of the time (i.e. the soul— by whatever name or aspect) but that it is in fact perceived at the same time as "wholly other" is one of the fundamental Odian paradoxes of human existence.

IV.
*Hailagaz

PGmc. *hail- has of course survived quite well as a word in English under ecclesiastical auspices as "holy," and in the verb form "to hallow," and the root also continues in the instructive words "hale," "hail," dialects in several categories of meaning:

1. "holy"— Go. hailags, OE hâlig, OFris. hêlich, OHG heilig, OS hêlag, ON heilagr.
2. "whole, healthy"— Go. hails, OE hâl, OFris. hêl, OHG heil, OS hêl, ON heill.
3. "health, happiness"— OE hæl, OHG heil, OS hêli, ON heill and heilsa.
4. "luck, omen"— OE hæl, hælo, OHG hailen, OS helian.
5. "to heal"— Go. hailjan, OE hælan, OHG heilen, OS hêlian.
6. "to greet"— OE hâlettan, OHG heillazzan, ON heilsa.
7. "to observe signs and omens"— OHG heilisôn.
8. "to invoke spirits, enchant"— OE hâlsian, ON heilla.

The basic adjectival concept of (temporary) well-being, invulnerability, becomes the nominal concept of "well-being" itself. This rather every-day complex, was however, naturally understood together with the forces which were thought to facilitate these blessings— therefore "luck" (a complex and profound concept in Germanic which is dealt with in Runelore), and in divinatory practice an "omen" signifying this luck. (From this the verbal concept in OHG heilisôn is directly derived.) The magical idea "to heal"—"to make whole, to make full of blessings" takes into account man's ability to hallow, i.e. to form a whole, "holy" thing by volition (cf. more on this together with *wîh- below). The greeting— ON heilsa! is the wish of well-being and wholeness for the person being greeted. When a vitki is in a state of wholeness with the world, and power dwells within his will, he is able to work his will in these realms, i.e. work his craft (which is in turn a "healing" activity). This explains the use of *hail- as a term for working magic.

*Hail- is that which takes part in the numinous quality which is blessed and whole, and which evokes the feeling of "wholeness" or "oneness" in the religious subject. It is generally that concept which met more favor among churchmen, as opposed to the more dynamic *wîh-.

V.

Although the two terms have been separated by history, we must again understand them as two parts of a single concept,— as they were to our forbears— inseparable and mutually dependent.

As we said above, this concept of the dichotomy of the holy is not unique to Germanic, and in fact is part of our Indo-European heritage. We can gain some insights into its working by examining some of the terms which we have inherited from Latin in English. The contrasting terms in Latin are *sacer* : *sanctus*. (in Greek they are 'αγιος : 'ιρος.) *Sacer* answers to *wîh* and *sanctus* to *hâlig*. From *sacer*, we have sacri-fice: "to make sacred," and that which is made sacred is the vic-tim (a semantic corollary with Germanic *wîh*). Something which is sanctified is holy, a part of the sacred by nature or by human volition. The two concepts can not exist without one another. That these contrasting terms belong organically together is evidenced by the fact that they are often juxtaposed to indicate the complete state or process of the holy. In English we preserve the Latin phrase: "sacrosanct." But we also find it in Germanic, e.g. in ON *vé heilakt* which answers perfectly to sacrosanct. That this is a common phenomenon to both, and not a borrowing, is shown by one of the most famous runic inscriptions (discussed in Runelore), the (Gothic) ring of Pietroassa. The last eight runes of the inscription appear:

These should be read *wîh-hailag*, again another perfect counterpart to "sancrosanct."

A thing is *wîhaz* as far as it belongs to, or has been made a part of the numinous, "otherly" realm (in a state of sacrality), and it is *hailagaz* in so far as this power resides in it and streams forth from it (for human benefit, etc.). So something must be *wîhaz* before it is *hailagaz*— the two are merely two functions of the same state or process. The general elimination of the living nature of the concept *wîhaz*— the dark, unknown and seemingly unknowable, unconscious side of the world and of the divinity which is evident in the Wild Hunt, the dark wood, the deep power of Wôden has led to a general deterioration of the ability of people to really perceive the holy in its entirety.

In the passive forms of religion (as opposed to the active, operant forms known as "magical"), this teaches us to honor and seek out the numinosum tremendum — despite the terror which we might have — for until one has "made friends with the horror" and learns from it— no true holiness may be engendered or experienced (at least not of the Odian kind). In active religion, where volition is brought to bear in order to either shape or to hold internal or external events, this dynamic dichotomy of the holy also has much to teach. In the archetypal, dynamic realm of the numinous there dwell real forces which constantly affect the conscious human realm. *Galdr* and *seiðr* represent the art and technique of communicating with these realms, and of receiving their corresponding communications in the form of conditions and experiences made conscious. Although we will speak more to the practical aspects of this theory in

Rune-Gild work, it should be clear that the object of what is called magic is to reach into the *wîhaz*-realm with a form intelligible to it that it may respond with *hailiz* — holiness — in some form. The holy is the externally attractive face of *wîhaz*, which is attractive because we see it most often "in our (external) image," however, the wîhaz behind it is often so "otherly" to us that it can be terrifying. However, in fact the wîhaz is deeply bound with our own inner-self, which is by definition impossible to know— since we (as inner-self) may never cease to be the subject and become the object (grammatically speaking) of our perceptions. This perception may only come in our communication with the hidden otherly "subject" in the numinous, where we can "come face to face" with that which is most like the truly imponderable, unknowable — inner self — the ultimate *numinosum tremendum*.

For more information on the idea of the holy in Germanic, see the two classic studies:

Baetke, Walter, *Das Heilige im Germanischen*. Tübingen: J.C.B. Mohr, 1942 and Hartman, Hans. *'Heil' und 'Heilig' im nordischen Altertum*. Heidelberg: Winter, 1943.

A RUNE OF HUGINN
(From *New Rûna*, No. 1)

For too long now there has been a dichotomy between the "rational" and "irrational" modes of investigation. We as Odians must seek out and employ a synthesis of these two modes. But in order to synthesize, one must first recognize and then develop the distinct characteristics of both equally— *solve et coagula*. The mistake of the past has been the result of the universalist, dualistic mentality which saw either of these two categories as "the truth," and the other as "mere delusion." Overdedication to either extreme has its inherent limitations, but the harmonious development of both has unbound potential for growth.

Everyday logic, or "common sense" is the ability to make decisions based upon objective facts, or as is many times the case with regard to the present topic, upon facts as far as they can be determined. It would be well worth the time of any student to pick up a basic textbook on logic and become more formally familiar with its techniques and language. Logic is valuable on several levels. In the social realm it makes one a more effective spokesman for his or her own views, and in the more personal and speculative-philosophical realm it may serve to build a more solid foundation for further work than could be gained by intuition alone.

Logic is the art of "hard" thinking, and making determinations based on criteria to which other "reasonable" persons might agree. This objectivist tendency is very close to all types of traditional thinking. In this regard traditionalists have a great advantage over the almost totally irrationally based adherents of revealed doctrines. However, as stated above, and as all strict objectivists will show, this approach only goes so far and as a result the objectivist is forced either to halt growth, or to give up objectivism to one degree or another. The true traditionalist does not have this problem, since his [omnijectivism] is a pragmatic outgrowth of a primary whole-consciousness model in which the objective : subjective dichotomy is an unarticulated feature. In this post-dichotomized age we may now analyze traditional thought as a way of beginning to return to it. Traditionalist "mystics" have always seen in manifest nature, that is, objectively observable phenomena, a real reflection of the field beyond the five senses, which can be built upon toward a deeper understanding of rune-realms. On the other hand, dogmatists of the school of revealed religion do not concede any reality to these phenomena and choose only to recognize certain "signs" in them placed here by some transcendent being to show the way to the "reality beyond." The traditional system is whole and forms a true bridge between the worlds of "rationality" and "irrationality," while the revelation doctrine is inherently dualistic in a real sense, and posits a gulf between the two modes. It is not hard to see why Christianity fought the growth of the human spirit for so many centuries, or how it used this gulf as a method of politico-psychological control.

Now, what is the relationship between these modes of intellectual activity in Odianism and what are the advantages of the synthetic approach? To begin with, it would be well to give the two modes personas that we may speak of them in more practical terms; the irrationalist we will call "the mystic," and the rationalist we will call "the scholar." These two modes or aspects (among others) need to be developed co-equally within the psychic complex of the Odian.

The mystic needs the scholar for two principal reasons, 1) to open interpersonal intellectual channels which provide for the spiritual "cross-fertilization," and 2) to find the openings to inner paths the entrances to which have often times been occulted by revelationist psychophysical conditioning. If the mystic intuits a formulation of any kind, and then "comes down from the mountain top," and demands that those below (who in no way participated in the intuition) accept his formulation, then he firmly places himself in the revelationist camp. However, if the intuition has been gained after traveling the road of observation [historical or natural], or if the mystic does not reveal his intuition before he retraces his steps along the road of observation charted by the intuition itself [and according to the laws of scientific scholarship], then he can begin to share the inspiration with others— "in their own language." This allows experiences to be shared, and provides the possibility for real constructive discussion (or if you will, argumentation). One scholar has the legitimate opportunity (and obligation) to say to the other either: "I agree, understand, or share your experience," or "I do not agree, understand, or share your experience," and furthermore he is able to state why this is the case. Again, there is a limitation in this paradigm since all must also recognize the often times subjectivity of truth.

On the second point: over the centuries we have been made the victims of a number of lies great and small, intentional and unintentional, which have conditioned our responses at all levels of our beings. One of the ways through these barriers can be the strict employment of objectivist criteria. In the realm of scholarship this can work in various ways. If Schliemann had acquiesced to "the common scholarly consensus" of his day Troy would still lie buried, and on the other hand, if the conquistadors had been more wise they would not have wandered aimlessly and perilously in search of their Eldorado. The objective search for clues may indeed lead the scholar to long hidden hoards of wisdom, the full force of which may not be assimilated by the objectivist means alone.

With regard to our own runic system, we have observed, and will continue to observe, how facts and clues dug out of the mass of evidence by hard scholarship can lead to doors which, if we had left to the fantasies [sometimes magically potent fantasies] of a bygone age, would have been passed over to this day.

In this age, the scholar also needs the mystic— the inspired master of intuition. The human spirit is now beginning to divest itself of the universalist mental yoke and is emerging into an age of the multiversalist melded mind. This new age must, however, be approached with discipline or we will merely again fall under the tyranny of an absolutist mental regime of the "rational" or "irrational" school— and there would be no growth in that.

Scholarship and science can reach a higher (that is, more effective) state of development if the possibilities of including the intuitive process and unorthodox procedures are given an institutionalized place in the work. The natural sciences, and especially physics, have begun to come to terms with this more effectively than have the humanities. This is understandable, since the humanities have long been subjected to extreme irrationalities from the full range of the ideological spectrum. Especially in the abstract fields of knowledge, a high degree of discipline with regard to the distinction between objective procedures and subjective methods — and the synthesizing of both — must be maintained. The objective analysis must occur in as pure a state as possible for it to be of maximal value in the final coagulation. All this makes the scholar of the humanities a more practically valuable member of society, since he or she becomes a viable part of the process of an evolutionary development of individuals and society. The correct analysis of archaic evidence becomes a practical and irreplaceable tool in the whole transformational process. The true scholar should function now — as he did in the Odian past — as a "shaman of the rational!"

In the final analysis our aim is the synthesis of what have recently been called "science" and "religion," and an ultimate end to the adverse relationship between the mystic and the scholar— in society and in the psyche of each individual on the Odian path. This can not be rightly done by the subjugation of any one of these to any other, but rather by an individuation — maximal development — of these elements (among others) in a model of consciousness in which the most noble aspects of all live harmoniously.

[Ed. Note: Many of these ideas have been up-dated in Edred's landmark essay "How to be a Heathen," published in *Idunna* (vol. 4, No. 4, December 1992, and subsequently improved and expanded in section II of the *Gildisbók*.]

An English Runo-Wôdenic Survival in the Middle Ages
(From *Rúna*, Vol. I., No. 1, Ostara, 1983)

The director on the Odinic Rite, Mr. John Yeowell, has recently produced a valuable little volume *Hidden Gods: The Period of Dual Faith in England, 681-1980*, which concerns the survival of Odinic ways in the age of mixed faith— a time in which we still to some extent live. Other books have also dealt with this subject, for example, E. Jung's *Germanische, Götter und Helden in christlicher Zeit* (München, 1939).

Wôden/Óðinn did indeed survive in many shapes and forms in supposed Christian lore and art, and in the art of the Middle Ages— in those times which were perhaps most militantly directed against Odinic wisdom (yet in which much of it was practiced!) Here, we would like to present a short study of a particular page of an obscure 13th century English manuscript found in Liège (MS Liège University Library [396 C1]). This page has a miniature of what appears to be a king with fiery streams flowing from his mouth into the mouths of five figures placed around the page.

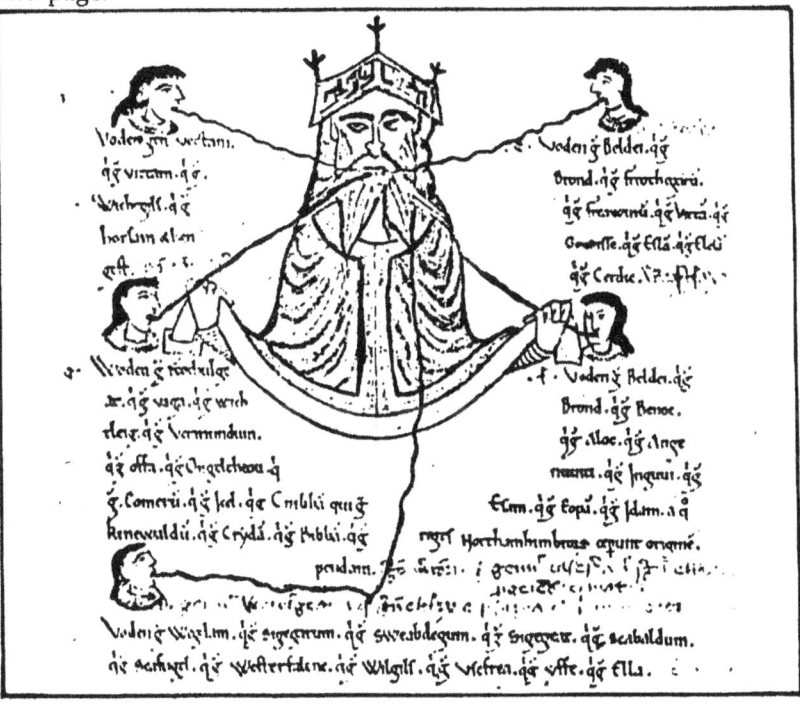

We are literally told by the Latin text that this figure is indeed Wôden or Voden— it is a text which describes the engendering of the English kings of Kent, Wessex, Mercia, Essex, and Sussex by Voden. The myth of the Wôdenic ancestry of the English kings is well known, and was well represented in medieval manuscripts— what is more interesting from the Odian point of view are both the crown, with its rune-like signs and the fiery streams.

Versions of a similar crown are not unfamiliar in other medieval manuscripts of the 11th-13th centuries— only they have *fleur-de-lis*— in the representation of Voden they are clearly runes. Here, it must be interjected that the Frankish *fleur-de-lis* symbol probably has a Germanic origin—and one that may be in common with that of the z-rune. The English certainly preserved knowledge of rune-lore and of the essential nature of the runes— even if it was syncretized with the lore of Christianity. Runes and runic Futhorcs continued to appear in English manuscripts into the 15th Century, and in the "Sawles Warde" we read: "ha witen alle Godes reades, his runes ..." = "they (= the Elect) know all god's purposes, (and) his secret councels..."

The staves mounted in the crown are three ᛉ PGmc. *Elhaz*: "elk"—or *algiz*: "protection." These are the swan-runes of the valkyries (OE *wælcyrie*)— the protective and wisdom-bringing beings of Wôdenic warriors, and of the cosmic harts in the boughs of the World-Tree. All in all, the ᛉ rune is a great symbol of the Wôdenic Way, as a sign of the connection between the divine and human realms.

As to the flames which emit from Wôden's mouth and enter into those of the kings of the five English realms mentioned on the page, they are clearly a graphic representation (as S.R.T.O. d'Ardenne. "A Neglected Manuscript of British History." In: *English and Medieval Studies*. London, 1962, pp. 84-93 also interprets them) of the "divine breath," of the spiritual quality and power which Wôden imparts to his descendants. The myth of the shaping of Askr and Embla in the *Prose Edda* (Ch. 9) and in the *Poetic Edda*, "Völuspá" 17-18, is also instructive. D'Ardenne points out that this symbology is of Germanic and not of Christian origin (p. 92) and indicates a parallel in which Havelock the Dane was recognized as heir to Birkabein because: "of his mouth it stod a stem/als it were a sunnebem; /also liht (= light) was it therinne (= there-in)/so ther brenden (= as though there were burning) cerges inne." The more ancient bracteates (about 450-550 CE) also often show a breath or flame emitting from the Wôdenic figure's mouth.

This evidence, coupled with all else we know of the early period of the mixed faith in England, leads us to the following conclusions:

    1. Detailed knowledge of the runes and of their connection with Wôden was maintained in England well into the "Christian Middle Ages"— this 500 to 800 years after the beginning of the Christianization process!— and —

    2. A fairly refined lore surrounding the All-Father, Wôden, was preserved— through oral traditions— among the English as late as the 13th century in a pagano-christian cultural context.

MORE ON THE LIÉGE WODEN-PAGE
(From *Rúna*, Vol. I., No. 2, Walburga, 1983)

Two further aspects of the ᛉ-rune and of the flame-breath of Wôden from this manuscript page which was previously discussed bear further treatment. Since this is from the Old English tradition, we would expect to be able to analyze the meaning of the ᛉ-rune from that tradition. As anyone who has studied the "Old English Rune Poem," and the Anglo-Saxon versions of the name of this rune can attest— it is a rough spot philologically speaking. In the Old English tradition, the recorded forms of the name which appear in various manuscripts include: iolx, ílx, ílcs, ílíx, with the standardized form being eolhx (with the phonetic value of [ks]). It seems clear that the original name of the rune was *elhaz OE *eolh*: "elk." Eolh-x may represent a contracted /-s/ suffixed, plural or genitive, form. The Rune Poem itself assigns the names *eolh-secg*: "elk-sedge"— a type of sharp-leafed swamp-grass. Other names which might have been attached to this rune are: *algiz*: "protection" (Go. *alhs*: "temple, sacred enclosure"), and ones which relate it to the Germanic Divine Twins, the Alcis (see Tacitus, Germania, ch. 43) and to the concept "swan" —> "swan maidens" (*valkyrjur*), see K. Schneider, *Die gemanischen Runennamen*, 1956. It is quite possible that all these meanings go back to a common root contained in the divine archetype of the Goddess of the Dawn flanked by two quadrapeds.

It is apparent that the runic emblems atop the crown of Wôden on the Liége manuscript represent something of the more esoteric meanings of the rune, which have to do with the connection of the divine realms to that of humanity, and the holy inviolate condition which comes about through this connection. It is therefore either an expression of the esoteric, magical function of *eolh-secg* (as being an apotropaic one), or of the value of the z-sign as one going back to some more archaic level of the runic tradition— one more archaic than that represented by the OE Rune Poem. It appears to me, from a Odian viewpoint, that the three elk-runes (numerical formulas $3 \times 3 = 9$, $3 \times 15 = 45 =$ NINE $\times 5$) express the vertical dynamism and striving of the Wôdenic way and as the essence of the royal cult of æthelings.

The fiery breath of Wôden also links up here, and it has its connection within the syncretic OE runic tradition. The name of the fourth rune in the OE row is *os*, which means "the god (*ansuz* = Wôden)" and in Latin it also means "mouth"— not irrelevant here since the "Old English Rune Poem" takes up this gloss and uses it as the rune-name itself. The triplectic god, Wôðanaz-Wiljôn-Wîhaz is a god of the word and the god who shapes Man in several stages or layers of action, among them the breathing of "spirit" (ON *önd*: "breath") into the newly shaped man and woman (Askr and Embla), see *Gylfaginning*, ch. 9 and the "Völuspá" sts. 17-18. This divine, fiery and vital breath constitutes the ongoing inspiration which Wôden gives to his descendants. But one must learn to breathe in this breath in order to get it. The motif of the vital breath of a Wôdenic figure goes back at least to the period between 450 and 550 CE where we see several bracteate depictions with a visible emission of breath, for example:

The vital breath is one means of gaining access to the mystery of the vertical striving of the ᛉ-rune.

RUNE-WISDOM AND RACE
(From *Rúna*, Vol. I, No. 2, Yule, 1982)

[Also published as "Who Will Build the Hearths of the Troth: Are Racial Considerations Appropriate?" in *Idunna* Vol. II, No. 2, July 1989.]

The question of "race" (an extremely ambiguous term) and its role in various aspects of the Neo-Germanic movement is complex and quite problematic. Almost every Germanic religious group has had to deal in some way with this matter. Our publications are filled with references to "racial" concerns. Much of this is of a healthy, positive nature (i.e. an effort to stake rightful claim to our heritage and pride in our traditions). But some fringe elements are often not quite so positive. A question one might ask is: why does the Neo-Germanic movement seem to be so preoccupied with this question (and not, for example, the Neo-Celtic)? This is not the place to enter into this precise, largely historical, question in any detail, but some light should be shed on it by rune-wisdom.

The racial question is primarily a socio-biological one, and one which is ultimately involved with the principles of group allegiance. The modern runers, inspired by Wôden and knowing the lore, should seek in the structural principles of allegiance practiced by our forbears— an elegant and dynamic system deserving of our loyalty today— the solution to this spiritual question. Too long has the revival of the elder ways of the Æsir floundered under the false and foreign doctrines of dualistically founded and negative "race hatred."

Before their "conversion" by the church, the ancient Germanic peoples owed their allegiances according to a structure best described by a set of concentric circles:

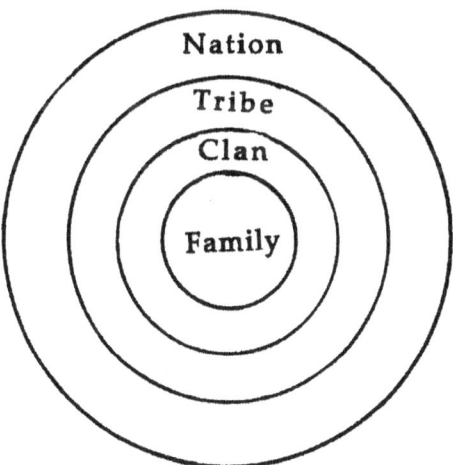

At the center of this scheme is the symbiotic relationship of individual to nuclear family— the primary allegiance of the individual. The secondary allegiance, but one closely bound to the first, is the clan (the word clan is from the Celtic *cland* or *clann*, which answers to the Germanic concept sib) or kindred, which the tribe (Ostrogoths, Vandili, Cherusci, etc., etc.) is quite tertiary, and the "nation" (i.e. "Germanic") was only a faintly conscious concept. The tribe is not, strictly speaking, a genetic construct, but rather an aggregation of clans held together for widely varying purposes by any one of a number of possible governmental institutions— all of which seek to integrate the kindred units into the whole tribal body. All this would seem to offer an ideal situation— one in which the ugly head of alienation could hardly raise itself. This structure describes the expression of the W-rune (*wunjô*: "joy")— which binds genetically descended beings together in a functioning organism— working through the more all-encompassing power of the O-rune (*ôpila*: "ancestral property")— which holds various structures together and preserves their integrity, while it allows "new blood" into the organism through ritual and sexual means.

An individual or group could quite easily be taken in and assimilated to any given "nation" or "tribe"— often through marriage (i.e. through the nuclear family) or through other ritual forms such as "blood brotherhood," or adoption. Whole groups could also be assimilated into a given tribal structure through religious or politico-military alliances. Examples of this process from the Migration Age would include the Gotho-Sarmatian symbiosis on the steppes of Western Asia (the Sarmatians were an Iranian people), and the assimilation of the Burgundians with the Huns (a Turkic people) which is faintly reflected in the Nibelungen saga, but which is best substantiated through archeological evidence. In later times the Slavo-Swedish symbiosis which led to the formation of the Kingdom of Kiev, and the work of Finns (Lapps) as accepted magicians in Scandinavia are good examples of the same process. In all this it is clear that although our (19th Century) concept "race" is most closely recalled by the term "nation" here, it is this "nation" or Volk concept which is most lacking in the genuine elder tradition. The concepts of family, kindred, and tribe held this branch of power for the ancient Germanic peoples— and these living organisms, their ways and traditions, could not be violated or compromised.

Theologically and cosmologically, this general or unconscious attitude (as it might best be described) is well reflected in the lore of the Germanic people. (This is discussed in some detail in the essay on esoteric theology in Runelore.) Many have broadly attempted to equate the "races" of gods, etins, etc., with the moral principles of Good and Evil, and then to equate these with the "races" of humanity— this approach was based upon a Manichean view— an ontologically dualistic philosophy (and the source of many negative aspects within Judaism and ultimately within Christianity). Some would have us believe that the gods and etins represent absolute-good and absolute-evil and that they are locked in mortal combat— the final outcome of which will be...? This whole view smacks not only of Zoroastrianism, but also of rampant Christianity in the souls of those who forward these ideas. Similar, but not identical, concepts may be held by kindred Thórists, but here we are speaking strictly to Odian *rúnar*. Without going into too much detail on this matter at present, it should always be realized that Óðinn is in fact the son of an etin-wife, Bestla, and that Þórr is her grandson and the son of an etin— Jörð (Earth). This ideological complex contains mysteries of the W-rune, and of the organically holistic nature of the H-rune and can be formulated into powerful themes for meditative work.

Not all of the mysteries are at once comprehended—but most can be understood by those with the will and wisdom to do so. It should not be assumed that the Rune-Gild posits a universalist creed or that it does not promote the importance of genetic descent with respect to the religion of the individual— although the story is vastly more complex than simple genetic descent. It merely sees this reality from a broader view. Ásatrú, by whatever name, is in our blood and the runes are our very breath. The "soul" and the "body" of each individual is bound together through time in a psychophysical complex. In part, we take an efficiency motivated approach with respect to the "choice" of religion, and opt for the eternal rather than the faddish answer.

Ásatrú is the faith which our forbears followed, unmolested by unnatural dreams and psychoses— it is encoded into our genetic structure and can never be removed. The schizophrenia from which the "West" suffers is largely the result of the attempt to graft the psychoses of Yahweh into the communal being of Ásatrú (and the other indigenous folk-ways of Europe). Therefore, when we are moved by "religious" or "magical" urges would it not be better, more efficient, to refer to the eternally valid book written within, rather than seeking after some exotic form of religion which has never had contact with our folk (i.e. ourselves in former modes of being)? This whole attitude is the natural outcome of an ideologically consistent form of pantheism. The *theos* or god involved must, however, be understood on the impersonal level of the *rún rúnanna*— the mystery of mysteries. All is god, god is all— so when seeking god seek that which you are. We are indeed the sum total of our ancestry — (= a genetic, linguistic, and cultural construct, see below) — which is a psychophysical reality— and one that can not be changed as one might change a shirt. The idea that one could do so was the folly of the churchmen.

The phenomenon of Ásatrú, and the power of the runes can not, however, be explained through a rudimentary and primitive 19th century racial ideology. Previous and present attempts to do so were and are doomed to failure because of their incomplete nature. Those of ancient Ásatrú had traditions, instinctive modes of behavior which insured their continuance in the stream of divine power— we must now re-integrate ourselves into it through a skillful combination of intuition and scientific knowledge, combined with the all important spirit or basic philosophical attitude which acts as a catalyst and regulator for the growth and development of our way.

Wôden's nature and function is one which synthesizes polar opposites from every corner of the multiverse into a whole. Thinking through this model can be a liberating experience, and one which should be the primary goal of every would-be Odian— each in his or her own way.

After having examined the genetic aspects of the old way, which form a part of our present philosophy— the "racial" (i.e. more correctly said the clanic) one— we now embark on a less discussed, but even more important aspect of the social features of Ásatrú. This involves the third of the rings of allegiance — the tribe — and the equally important fifth ring which even in ancient times could supersede them all— the band. (The Germanic word "band" is used here in the sense of association— i.e. retinues (warrior bands), cultic bands, gilds— originally sacrificial associations— fellowships, etc., etc.) The family and the clan are unmistakably genetic, and so the familio-clanic features of religion (household cult) are strongly shaped by this model. That of the fourth, hazy, ring, the "nation," or "race" as our too often 19th century minds sometimes understand it, is fairly unconscious, but it gives the basic outlines of religious conception and this is often most apparent in the divine nomenclature.

The tribe is the principal institution in which religious cult found its highest expression. It is the tribal context in which the great sacrificial rituals and festivals take place and it is the tribal religion which finds reflection in myth and epic (although the "national mythology" may share many archetypes and even mythic paradigms). Tribes which share an important cultic feature and which live in close proximity to one another may form a religious amphictyony— i.e. they come together to celebrate their common cult on special occasions. The Ingvaeones ("the people of Ing") were probably such a group, as were the Continental Saxons (the people of the sax-sword).

From the "racial" point of view, the thing that is most important to realize about the tribe is that as an institution it is super-genetic. It is not dependent upon genetic descent but upon belonging to a religio-political union, bound together by a common mythology (i.e. idealized paradigms of action) and purpose. The tribe is not a super-extended clan— or very rarely is. Often one ancient clan, characterized by their "totem animal" or divine ancestor would place their stamp upon a tribe even after the original clan had died out and been replaced by new groupings, e.g. the Wylfings ("descendants of the wolf"), Gautar (Goths) = "descendants of Gaut" (= Wôden). But more often the tribal names reflect the concept of a union of clans, e.g. Alemanni ("all-the-people"), Franki ("people of the *franca*"— a kind of spear), Markomanni ("people of the borderland"). Tribes are usually formed by a voluntary action of several clans, who then proceed to live beside one another, intermarry, develop a common cult and myth, and share their fate. This more accurate picture of tribal development holds out the hope of the possibility of a new tribalization in the West because it separates the tribal concept from a strict and stale genetic model (which was probably inherited from Hebraic mythology). These concepts have been most completely developed by Reinhard Wenskus in his monumental study, *Stammesbildung und Verfassung: Das Werden der frühmittelalterlichen gentes* (Köln: Böhlau, 1961).

The fifth ring, that of the band, holds out even more hope for the genuine re-traditionalization of Ásatrú, and one upon which the Rune-Gild is naturally formed. The band-construct is one based upon the coming together of individuals for a specific long-term purpose and the institutionalization of this grouping through a common ritual (including initiation), mythology, and ethic. These individuals may be drawn from all quarters and are held together and develop according to a pattern best described as an aristocracy of merit. This system was already being used in Indo-European times for war-expeditions and cultic practice. In this basic construct, which took on many forms throughout history and is ultimately responsible for the shape of most of our institutions in the West today, a leader (who has no inherent powers, but only those lent to him/her by virtue of demonstrated ability by the body of qualified members)— this in the case of the (non-standing) warrior-band which also finds expression in the (standing) retinue around a king — or around a set of leaders — this in the case of cultic bands or the gilds which developed out of the cultic sphere, undertake to educate, train, and maintain a coherent body of members with a complex tradition. This is an almost universal pattern of human activity, but one which has been little studied in its own right. The fundamental organizational principle is a three leveled hierarchy, e.g. the page, knave, and knight; the apprentice, journeyman, and master; the baccalaureus, magister, and doctor, etc. The loyalties generated in these extra-genetic bands always superseded the familial ones— this conflict of loyalties is the centerpiece of one of the most important Indo-European epic motifs: the father-son battle (cf. Hildebrant and Hadubrant in the *Hildebrantslied*—in which the son is sworn to defend the border of his land for his king, and the father is bound to regain the kingship taken from him.)

Therefore, we see three types of traditional organizational institutions:

1. the familial (genetic)
2. the tribal (geneto-voluntary)
3. the associative (non-genetic, voluntary)

Ásatrú itself may be said to belong to the first two, while the Rune-Gild belongs to the third.

The band-construct is as viable today as it was millennia ago; through it we can "revive" much in a purely traditional way. However, the more "religious" aspect — that much discussed concept of folk-religion — is in need of a more refined and elegant construct for revival. To these ends the esoteric methodology of the "high-holy-three" may be applied in order to uncover a viable pattern of Ásatrú/Odinist traditional revival. The genetic, or metagenetic, argument is powerful, and we have tried to articulate it in the first part of this article— but it has its definite weaknesses in a revivalist scheme. Principal among these is that carried to its logical conclusion it ends in a equation of "racial purity" and "divine contact." For if we say that someone is in contact with the Germanic gods because they are mainly of Germanic descent, then we could end in arguing that because someone else (anyone else) has more Germanic blood then he is automatically more in contact with these archetypes. The ultimate conclusion of such a simplistic and static reasoning would quite obviously be absurd, and what is more, not very convincing. To this important metagenetic, biological line we must add other factors, 1) language, and 2) culture, in order to come up with a complete rationale for Germanic revivalism. Language is a paradigmatic mind-set which encodes the psyche of all who speak it with certain conceptual modes and possibilities. People who have a Germanic language as their Mother Tongue (i.e. English, German, Dutch, or any of the Scandinavian dialects) and who have grown up in cultures formulated by Germanic traditions and thought may also be impressed with the spirit of Ásatrú/Odinism. Culture is a complex sociological mixture of all that goes into the life of a people, and encompasses both the concepts of ancient cultural continuity and environmental influence. It seems that a deeper and more convincing explanation of the Ásatrú/Odinist phenomenon might be sought in this conceptual triangle:

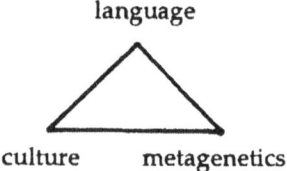

In this article we have tried to articulate an approach to the concept of community which is based on the three traditional Germanic models of family, tribe and band. All are necessary to a healthy growth of the faith, but each must be developed in its own way. Through this, it is hoped that a good deal of light has been shed on the curious "problem" of racialism in the Germanic revival.

Taking the traditional Odian viewpoint on the subject, and one reflected in Germanic history (until very modern times at least), it would seem that this should be regarded as "the problem that never should have been." The "racial question" which so heavily dominated the early phases of Germanic revivalism should for the most part be tempered in the pursuit of future development. The principle of the Odian Paradox and the ultimate synthetic nature of the archetype in possession of the runes leads us to govern our philosophical stand on this matter from a broad plane— the Odian often sees this question with no little humor.

Since "race" was never a real category of allegiance for the ancients, why should it be one now? As Odians our allegiance is owed to our biological families (be they Ásatrú or not), to our kindred (which has taken the place of our tribe), and to our band (Varangian Guard, Rune-Gild, etc.). This model would seem to be more in keeping with Germanic tradition, and the rune-lore expressed in the formula ..., than the 19th century natio-racial model. What is more, from a magical point of view, the nationalist model invariably seems to lead to a primary motivation in the destruction of some opposing racial and/or military foe which somehow seems the "key" to future development. Such constructs are doomed to failure because the enduring desire (= binding force) for destruction will naturally be drawn to its source. This is not morality, but a psycho-magical function (which individuals can often bypass, but which groups can almost never avoid). When the ancients had an enemy which they had to destroy, they normally entered into the task with one of two psychic attitudes, 1) one of battle-ecstasy, or 2) one of a deep sense of duty. A careful reading of history and saga will show this to be the case. Those runemasters who are able to control the magical power of hate do so within strict technical and ritual limitations.

Further, it is hoped that this paper has shown some of the ways rune-wisdom may be applied to certain problems and matters of social and/or philosophical concern— by using a combination of subjective, intuitive inspiration with objective observation of the historical record of tradition. As for the importance of the views outlined above in a program of personal development: principally, it should help serve as a catalyst for thought, and possibly as a guide to certain aspects of the world. A realistic and healthy view of the cosmos and of human society is a necessary step in the balanced growth of the Runer.

A Brief History of German Runic Esotericism
(From *The Runestone*, No. 41, Fall, 1982)

[Ed. Note: The subject of this article has been further expanded and explored by Edred in his book *Rune Might: Secret Practices of the German Rune Magicians* (Llewellyn, 1989.).]

In this article we will sketch a brief history of German runic esotericism, to which the *Armanen Orden* is heir. More detailed outlines of this fascinating history, and of the men and women who shaped it— will be published in future works of the Rune-Gild.

It must be noted that reliable information is often hard to come by in this field, as one is always dependent upon sometimes ambiguous primary texts combined with secondary sources from strongly antagonistic pro and con interest groups.

The real beginning of the runic wave in central Europe came in Austria, with the publication of *Das Geheimnis der Runen* ("The Secret of the Runes") by Guido von List in 1908.* In the years between 1908 and his death in 1919 at the age of 71, von List published a series of works through a society built up around his personality— the *Guido-von-List-Gesellschaft* (founded in 1905 in Vienna).

Before the beginning of the "Guido-von-List-Society," von List had been greatly influenced by the ideology of the Theosophical Society. After a cataract operation in 1902, his eyes were bandaged for several months, during which he received "a magical initiation." The "secrets of the runes" were revealed to him and he henceforward dedicated himself to the restoration of *Armanentum* in a Pan-Germanic cultural and mystical context. Between 1904 and 1919, Guido von List produced a series of works which outlines his philosophy and mystical thought. The final work in this series, *Die Kabbala und die Esoterik des Armanismus* ("The Kabbala and Armanic Esotericism), mysteriously never appeared. Rumors abound to this day about the whereabouts of the missing manuscript.

The form of von List's runology was briefly out lined in the first installment of "Rûna", in the article entitled "The Fuþark." It is the belief of the *Armanen* that the 18-rune row is the primal one, and the heritage of ancient "Arctogea."

Although the foundation of a formal esoteric branch of the society was planned, no actual magical work appears to have been done by von List (This according to Adolf Schleipfer, present Grand Master of the *Armanen Orden* and President of the Guido-von-List-Gesellschaft, in an undated personal communication).

After List's death, the work of the society and the publication of the Master's literature were continued— until between 1933 and 1937/38 when the society was outlawed and repressed by the National Socialists. A core group was able to survive the war years, however, and ultimately able to pass the heritage of *Armanentum* on to younger hands in the 1960s.

List was the great founder, but many others went their own way. Principal among these was the Frisian-born Friedrich Bernhard Marby. Marby was a true practicing esotericist— a magician, if you will. The

---

* Translated into English as *Secret of the Runes* by Stephen E. Flowers (Destiny, 1988).

highly effective technique of "rune gymnastics" was developed, or rather **rediscovered**, by him as early as 1907. At the root of "Runen-Gymnastik" is the idea that the runes originated from simple forms of human bodily postures which in turn were expressions of inner psychic charges. The runic postures can be used to invoke these energies and the human body becomes a sender/receiver for streams and waves, chthonic and cosmic, in combination with the correct singing ("rowning") of rune-words and names. This practice of this system was detailed in his four-volume "*Marby-Runen-Bücherei*" which was first published between 1931 and 1935.

A reputed student of Marby who went his own way was Siegfried Adolf Kummer. Essentially, Kummer practiced the same technique of "runic gymnastics" as Marby, and published two major works, *Die heilige Runen-macht* ("The Holy Rune-Might," in 1932) and *Runen-Magie (1933/34). He also founded the *Runenschule Runa* ("Rune-School Runa") in 1927 near his home city, Dresden.

Both Marby and Kummer were primarily interested in esoteric, magical matters, and were somewhat less concerned with social and political questions. Both were, however, possessed of a racial ideology which was part and parcel of the Nordic Renaissance of early 20th century Germany. They wanted not only to transform the individual, but also their entire folk.

The wide esoteric neo-Germanic wave, of which Marby, Kummer and the Guido von List Society were important parts, and the more popular cultural and religious wave represented by the "Teutonic Faithful Community," and many other groups were all manipulated and twisted by the National Socialists to their political ends. The result was the outlawing and repression of the organizations from which the NSDAP (the National Socialists) had filched most of their more popular propaganda, and the eventual destruction of many of the people involved. Some died on the battle fronts, some in concentration camps. Kummer apparently did not survive, and Marby had to spend 99 months, between 1936 and 1945, in Dachau.

The Nazis themselves left us very little in the way of true esoteric runology. For them, the runes were a kind of "magic"— but only of a manipulative, not transformational, kind. Appealing runic or rune-like images could be used, and were used, to inspire both terror and reverence. In the end the National Socialists did more to destroy the credibility and progress of the great new Germanic wave than all the Bolsheviks and Zionists combined. We are just now, we hope, emerging from their shadow.

After the war, Marby began to rebuild what had been taken from him. His books were republished and he began to gather students again. At about the same time, another esoteric runologist, **Karl Spiesberger, emerged on the scene. Spiesberger's philosophy is fundamentally different from Marby's, since he professes an eclectic "Pansophy" while Marby essentially belongs in the "Ariosophic" camp (The term Ariosophy is an ethno-ethical construction, especially used by Jörg Lanz von Liebenfels,

---

* This text has been published in English by Rûna-Raven Press (1993).
** Spiesberger's background lies more with the *Fraternitas Saturni*. For an overview of this group see S. Flowers' *Fire and Ice* (Llewellyn, 1990).

based on the two more well-known esoteric "sophies" of the era: Theosophy and Anthroposophy). Spiesberger's two main runic works are *Runenmagie* (1955) and *Runenexerzitien für Jedermann*. Both are still in print in new editions.

In 1966, F.B. Marby died, and with him an era. Although the first phase of the saga of the Northern Dawn in Germany had been told, there was a second phase to be begun— which might be said to have commenced in 1966. By 1968, the Guido von List Society had gotten a new president in the person of Adolf Schleipfer and work was begun to refound the *Armanen Orden*. New directions were given to old institutions. As an organic, growing body it had burst forth from its seed-life into the light of day.

THE *ARMANENSCHAFT*
(From *The Runestone*, No. 40, Summer 1982)

 The *Armanen* runic system is the vigorously practiced runic tradition of present-day Germany. The *Armanenschaft* is a comprehensive religio-magical system and community (composed of members of the Guido-von-List-Gesellschaft— a kind of outer organization and of the *Armanen Orden*, AO, itself— the inner ring). Many readers may be somewhat familiar with the person of Guido von List, the founder of this tradition. However, most of the information heretofore available concerning his work has been rather sensationalized (e.g. *The Spear of Destiny*) or all too brief, as in the *Encyclopedia of the Unexplained*, etc. With this short article I cannot hope to fill the gaps concerning this important figure in the Northern Renaissance; nevertheless, it would seem that a sympathetic first-hand report concerning the group dedicated to his vision might be beneficial in this regard.
 I was able to attend a day of the three day Herbst Thing held by the *Armanenschaft* (10-31 - 11-01-1981 e.v.). During this time, and through correspondence, I was able to build a working relationship between myself and the Rune-Gild, and the leadership of the *Armanenschaft* and the AO— to the extent I am sure their knowledge will, in the future, constitute a continuous fertilization of new ideas and elements in the work of the Rune-Gild. The scene was a magnificent ruined castle (the Gleiberg) on a high hill outside Giessen, Germany. This was most assuredly a cultic (probably juridical) site in ancient times— as is graphically shown by the now only intermittently intact Gleiberger Weg which leads to the castle from town, and which is lined with linden trees (a symbol of juridical power in ancient Germania).
 The Thing-Conference, which was well attended by around 100 persons, most of whom were members and all of whom were solid supporters of the *Armanenschaft*, consisted of a vital combination of talks on various topes of philosophical and theological interest (e.g. "The Myths of the Forces of Darkness in the Germanic Religion: Loki, Fenris-wolf, the Midgard-serpent, Hel and the Giants and their meaning for us"), folk dancing, dynamic skaldic recitations, and ritual activities (both closed and open to those outside the inner ring of the AO). The activities were held in a highly atmospheric hall, adorned with the symbols of the *Armanenschaft* and dominated by an altar ruled over by an image of Wodan and a magnificent wooden representation of the Irminsûl— the focus of this Thing was the Odinic Self-Sacrifice.
 This Odinic Self-Sacrifice was paradigmatically realized through a magico-religious rite, which involved the sacrifice of horse-flesh, bread and mead. The ritual climax was skillfully built up throughout the entire day. The day began with a philosophical lecture concerning the *Armanen* nature of a line of particularly German thought from the Middle Ages to the 20th century entitled, "The Great Germans." This was followed by a bout of vigorous Vanic folk dancing to ring out the Summer in honor of the Sun. These dances involved almost everyone at one point or another, and seemed to fulfill their ancient functions of intensifying and raising the level of sexual polarities and energy. The Vanic dancing was concluded with sometimes didactic and often dramatic skaldic recitals. This included the

complete recitation from memory — by the might of Muninn — of the "Grímnismál" by one of the brothers— to the honor of the All-Vater.

The great Sacred Rite "Wodan's Sacrificial Death" was a thought-provoking, moving, exciting, inspiring and energizing experience. Without revealing the details of the rite, it may be said that it consisted of a series of poetic invocations and songs calling the might of Wodan. This also included runic exercises to build up the energy in the folk present at the Thing— all intermixed with periods for reflection and meditation to powerful Wagnerian themes and *Also Sprach Zarathustra*. It might be noted that the invocations and readings were performed by a wide variety of the members of the AO present, and other cultic roles were also fulfilled by a number of *Armanen*. The presence of *wôd* could certainly be felt in the hall, and seemed embodied in its master— Wôdan. In order to take part in the giving of self to self a consecrated ritual meal of horse flesh, mead, and bread was taken in stillness...

The *Armanen Orden/Guido-von-List-Gesellschaft* was re-formed and re-founded in 1969 by the present Grand Masters, Adolf and Sigrun Schleipfer, after the long interregnum between the death of GvL in 1919 and the eventual dissolution of the society during World War II and the return of more hospitable times. It does seem that the end of the 7th and the beginning of the 8th decade of our century was the era of foundations for our movement in general. According to the leadership of the High Armanen Order (HAO) itself, GvL did not die without "having left behind a complete RITUAL for the AO." There can be little doubt that this Order represents one of the most powerful movements for inner awakening of Germanic consciousness in the world today.

PERSONAL AUTHORITY AND ODIAN ETHICS
(1980)

> This article was originally written sometime during 1980 and was to be included in the old *Lore-Books*, but as the book *Runelore* (Weiser, 1987) superseded the *Lore-Books*, this little work just fell through the cracks. It is produced here for the first time for the sake of having a complete record of the ideas housed within the Gild. Edred.

It is our main purpose in this offering to discuss the meaning of ethics, that is, responsibility to self and to others in the Odian Way. Here we can only hope to partially cover this topic with regard to Odianism and Gild-Work, and it does not begin to cover the over-all questions of ethics within the Ásatrú/Odinist community as a whole. However, some of what we have to say here is certainly relevant to the clarification of dark corners of the ethos of the Troth.

First, we should clarify our terms. A somewhat artificial distinction can be made between the ideas of *morals* and *ethics*. We could say that morality is that which is imposed from the outside, and ethics is that which is that which is developed from within. This is artificial because in Indo-European the concept of which we speak can only be thought of as something coming from *within*, what belongs to one's self or inner being. "Moral" ultimately goes back to a PIE root *me-, which means "an inner quality of mind"— our related word in English would be "mood." While "ethical" goes back to third person and reflexive pronoun root *seu-, "that which belongs to one's self." (The Greek *ethnos*: "creed" and *ethos*: "folk" go back to the same root— which speaks volumes in and of itself.) The Christian church introduced a non-organic, externally imposed morality, which posed a right and a wrong based on a prescribed set of inflexible divine laws, said to originate in some transcendent state. Only the high priests, popes, imams and the like had access to it, of course. All of this is only one aspect of the use of *custom* as a manipulative tool of the politics of power used by the church in its early years to subvert the ethics of the folks of the world. In the hearts of all there remained the inner sense of right and wrong, and the psychic tension which has developed between this inner sense and the externally imposed one has been the greatest source of guilt (both cultural and individual), and inner as well as outer conflict for the last few hundred years.

A moral philosophy is based upon a true and real (ontological) dichotomy between good and evil as applied to daily action. Moralistic philosophies, such as the revealed religions (Judaism, Christianity, Islam) have, perceive a strict dichotomy in the world, and call one *a priori* eternally "good" and one "evil." Furthermore, this distinction is made on *moral* grounds— determined by "higher authority." The historical question as to how well this concept ever caught on psychologically in the West is not our topic— but the answer seems clear. However, for the Odian, the dichotomy between any two poles is merely the tool toward the re-assimilation of the opposites— light and dark, soul and body. The Odian does not deny or try to destroy one for the sake of the other, but rather attempts to develop both to their ultimate potential. Therefore, by definition, Odianism is an "amoral" philosophy. This is why the Odian Way is only meant for a few in our community. This does not mean that

Odianism is a hedonistic philosophy — on the contrary — it must always be a strictly disciplined path of action. But these actions are governed by the voice of "inner rede," a deep level of the self which gives council as to what that path must be. Winning contact with the voice of one's fetch is one of the objects of the training undertaken by siblings of the Gild. Once this "inner rede" has been reached, and one's destiny (wyrd) has been learned, a path is shaped and made known— straying from this path is to do wrong, the steady advancement on that path is to do right. The way can only be fully determined within the individual according to his or her total being. One of the purposes of the tradition is to show the methods of obtaining this inner rede— the way to knowledge of one's own wyrd.

Within the entire complex of the Troth, the ethical characteristics of Odianism may be meaningfully contrasted with those of Thorism. This is most obvious in the relationships the gods Óðinn and Þórr have with the etins. Þórr, although he is the "grandson" of an etin, is rightfully their sworn enemy— for it is his organic function to protect the realm of Asgard from their encroachment. Þórr must never ask himself: "Should I kill this etin, or should I engage him in conversation about his origins and what wisdom he might possess?" He is only to strike with Mjöllnir and ask questions later. However, Óðinn as often as not visits the etins in order to obtain knowledge from them— although they might be adversaries on one level they nevertheless have a certain respect for one another. Þórr is moralistic, he has "been taught" (it is "in his blood") that he is to recognize etins and their forces and destroy them, while Óðinn is amoralistic— he sees the ultimate wholeness of all, recognizes the larger multiversal reality which partakes of all worlds.

Odian ethics are therefore true to the Law of the Whole. Although they may fairly be characterized as Selfish, it is, of course, a Holy Self which is intended. The Odian is always dedicated to four things which govern his or her path: 1) the Self, 2) the Kindred, 3) Consciousness in the Multiverse, and 4) the idea of the dynamic synthesis of polar opposites within the whole.

The Rune-Odian recognizes the multiversal aspects of the Self and it is always his or her will to develop that Self in accordance with inner rede. In this area **good** is that which strengthens the Self, the higher (more whole, or integrated— in Jungian terms "individuated") *ego*— "I." This is the "I" which is used in many of the ancient magical runic inscriptions which begin: *ek* (= "I") + a holy name or title identifying that "I" as a kind of integrated "magical persona." *Evil* is that which leads to a disintegration. But since there are as many paths as travelers it is next to impossible to judge your fellow "vagabonds of the soul."

Another side of this view, and an important ethical consideration, is service to the Kindred. Óðinn's quests for wisdom are almost always undertaken in the service of gods and men— to increase their powers of inspiration and to open wider the doors of consciousness. Even his apparent untrustworthiness can be understood from this angle. Óðinn is not bound by any law in his quests. Any guise, any work is right if it suits his larger noble purpose— he could easily be called the *Übergott!* However, the basic message for Odians here is: *Share* what you have learned, or the benefits of what you have learned and gained, with your Gild-Fellows. The Way of Óðinn is not the path of the hermit or monk!

With regard to what was said above about the relationship of Óðinn with the etins, it must be remembered that although Óðinn has given himself to the growth of synthetic consciousness, he uses this power — with all his might — to hold cosmic order in its balance, and to avoid (or delay) at all costs the coming *ragnarök*. A Odian can not therefore be in any way a nihilist, and must be dedicated to the preservation of consciousness, of natural order, and cosmic balance. (All three of which are *not* the same thing!)

Finally, all of these sometimes seemingly contradictory elements must be synthesized into a Whole model within the individual psychophysical complex, and then harmoniously find its place within the greater multiversal complex.

The Odian Way is a difficult path, and it is not suitable for most because only a fool of a sort would chose it. It has long been recognized as a noble calling, and we seem to be in great need of the ideas of Odianism at this nascent stage of the Dawn of the Gods — for it is Óðinn who is the shaper — the formulator and projector of works and words. It is in his power that the light of the new dawn shall have its beginnings, and through his form that the rays shall shine forth— just as that power first shaped the world, so now and forever it will re-shape it.

LANGUAGES
(From *New Rûna*, No. IV)

This text has been substantially revised and expanded for this Second Revised Edition of *Green Rûna*.

Languages are to the humanities what mathematics are to the natural sciences. Every member of the Rune-Gild should ideally engage him or herself in an organized program of learning languages other than English which will be a help in the study of esoteric Germanic lore. This will be of practical benefit, since new sources of information (much more vast than anything available in English) will open up, and of psycho-mental benefit, because this activity is an invaluable well-spring of intellectual exercise. If one is able to undertake the serious study of a language in which primary sources of runelore (principally Old Norse) is written, then a new conceptual world may be broken open, to reveal the eternal ideological rune-hoard within.

The learning of languages has been a part of the Germanic initiatory system since ancient times. When Sigurðr was fostered to the dwarf Reginn, the wise old wight taught the young hero three things initially: 1) the game of *tafl* (a board game), (2) the lore of the runes (the exoteric side— the esoteric side he learns from Sigrdrífa), and 3) the speaking of many tongues which may be interpreted as both the Germanic dialects (so that he could communicate across tribal boundaries) and the poetic languages of the worlds as described in the Eddic lay the "Alvíssmál."

This article is intended to set forth this concept, and to help guide the learner in the direction best suited for his or her individual situation.

There are essentially two types of languages to be considered: what might be called secondary languages, that is, those modern languages in which works about the old traditions have been written (especially in the last 200 years), and primary languages, that is, those older dialects in which we have extant manuscripts which more directly reflect the traditions themselves. Some languages may be considered to belong to both categories, as we will see below.

When considering the language learning plan best suited for you, you should take several things into account: 1) how much time do you have to spend on it?, 2) how many languages do you already know and what are your general linguistic abilities?, and 3) what are the formal (that is, class-room) opportunities in your geographical area? From what is said below, you should be able to get a picture of what type of program you could design for yourself.

Secondary Languages

Among the most useful modern languages, the most available in a formal setting is German— and it is definitely the most utilitarian language for scholarly secondary literature. Also, many primary works of the Neo-Germanic movement (for example, the words of Guido von List and current publications of the *Armanen Orden*) are written in this language. German is, of course, no easy language, but it can be fairly painlessly acquired in thousands of classroom settings in this country and in Germany. With this, as well as all the other modern languages, self-study is an option— but generally a poor one it would usually seem. If at all possible enroll in some formal class. The best general series of self-study books is provided by the Teach Yourself Books— which has titles on all the modern languages discussed here, as well as Old English. Finally, let it be said that German does require a good deal of effort— but its practical rewards are well worth it.

The Scandinavian languages are an intellectual bargain for the English speaker. As opposed to German (with a complex verbal and case system, and sometimes tortuous syntax) the Scandinavian dialects are very similar to English and are often more simple. Also, once you have solidly acquired one of the three European Scandinavian dialects (Norwegian, Danish, or Swedish) you have virtually de facto acquired reading knowledge of the other two because they are so similar. The only drawback is the relative rarity of places in which these languages are formally taught, and the resultant rarity of many of the important works in the libraries. However, the fact that they are somewhat less complex, and the learner will be able to progress much faster with self-study than he or she would be able to with German is a plus in that direction.

In passing, we might also mention for those who know, or are learning French, there are a good deal of secondary works in that language— especially on mythology and religious history (for example, Dumézil, Eliade, Mauss, van Gennep) and runology (e.g. Musset).

Finally, among the modern languages we come to the bridge of tongues— Icelandic. As most readers probably know already, modern Icelandic is virtually unchanged from the language spoken in the Viking Age— a single page of orthographic and phonetic rule changes fills the narrow gap of centuries. Therefore, the student has the unprecedented opportunity to learn a "classical," primary language as a living modern tongue. Although this opportunity is quite rare in formal settings. There is, however, an excellent, if expensive, course put out by Linguaphone. (Write to International Learning Systems, 1753 Connecticut Ave., N.W., Washington, D.C. 20009 for details.) Also, the reader probably does not have to be informed that Icelandic (and hence ON) is quite difficult— on a level of complexity substantially beyond that of German. It is not to be undertaken with a light heart.

Primary Languages

Before taking on a primary language, which usually requires more time and personal effort in order to acquire any proficiency, it is advisable that one have a background in a modern language of similar difficulty and structure, for example, German. Perhaps Old English is the exception here— after all it is ENGLISH! But in any case, the method of learning these languages, even in the formal setting (which is rare and usually only in graduate schools of major universities) is virtually one of self-teaching.

A valuable aid in the preliminary study of the primary languages is a book by Orrin W. Robinson entitled *Old English and its Closest Relatives: A Survey of the Earliest Germanic Languages* (Stanford University Press, 1992). The subtitle is most descriptive here. The book does not focus especially on Old English, but is a general survey of all the older Germanic dialects with some grammatical commentary and sample texts from each. It is the only book in English of its kind.

With regard to these older languages it seems most beneficial to provide a rudimentary bibliography of learner's grammars and a word on the nature of the texts available in each language.

Old Norse

For ON, Gordon, E.V. *An Introduction to Old Norse.* Oxford: Clarendon Press, 1974, 2nd ed. (Introduction to literature, anthology of texts, grammar, glossary), is a classic and quite convenient beginning. Also recommended, but sometimes hard to acquire is *Old Icelandic: An Introductory Course* by Sigrid Valfells and James E. Cathey (Oxford, 1981). This latter book has self-tutorial lessons, but is also heavily laden with linguistic theory and lacks a substantial reader.

There are thousands of pages of Old Norse texts in existence, some having never been translated. This is, of course, by far the most valuable single primary language to the deeper understanding of the inner worlds of Northern thought housed in its linguistic structures.

What is most recommended is that the student of ON learn *Modern Icelandic* as a living language. The rules indicating the differences between modern Icelandic and Old Icelandic are so few they can be printed on a single page. Icelandic is the one "classical" language which can be said to still be a fully *living language.*

Old English/Anglo-Saxon

OE is also sometimes also popularly called Anglo-Saxon. There are many good beginning texts. Among them are Cassidy, F.G. and R.N. Ringler, eds. *Bright's Old English Grammar and Reader.* New York: Holt, Rinehart, and Winston, 1971, 2nd ed. (grammar, texts, glossary), and Moore Samuel and T.A. Knott. The Elements of Old English. Ann Arbor: Wahr, 1971 (grammar, texts, glossary). There are no purely pagan texts in OE, but much of the poetic corpus (including the *Bêowulf,* riddle literature, and the OE Rune Poem) contain overwhelmingly heathen conceptions. The chief advantage to learning OE for modern English speakers lies in the deep insight it gives into their own particular linguistic heritage and the links it provides with the ancient Germanic past. It is thus most organically connected to our present deep-ideological structure.

However, what is most recommended for those interested in the pursuit of Old English is the course offered though *Þâ Engliscan Gesiþas* (the English Companions)— a society based in England the purpose of which is the pursuit of Anglo-Saxon culture. They have a correspondence course in Anglo-Saxon (Old English) for their members with tapes and lessons. This course approaches Anglo-Saxon as a *living language,* and hence the student can *internalize* the language much more effectively. For our purposes this is imperative. The mailing address of *Þâ Engliscan Gesiþas* is: The Membership Secretary, *Þâ Engliscan Gesiþas,* Box 4336, London, WC1N 3XX, England.

Old Saxon

Closely related to Anglo-Saxon, Old Saxon is the old dialect of the form of German spoken in the far northern part of that country. The two major texts in the older language are the *Heliand,* a "novelized," and Germanicized, account of the life of "Chieftain Jesus," and a short fragment of a "translation" of Genesis. Most of the instructive material on this somewhat obscure dialect are found in German, e.g. F. Holthausen's *Altsächsisches Elementarbuch* (Winter, 1921).

Old Frisian

The Frisian dialect is still spoken in the regions of far eastern Holland and the adjacent region in Germany— Ostfriesland. Thomas Markey's *Frisian* (Mouton, 1981) is the only recent work in English covering the language. There are no epics in Old Frisian, but ther are a great number of law texts, which give significant insight into the legal, and hence cosmological views of these culturally very conservative people.

Old High German

For those who already know modern German fairly well, this can be learned with a modicum of difficulty. But about the only English learner's guide is that of Wright, Joseph. *An Old High German Primer.* Oxford: Clarendon Press, 1906 (grammar with texts, including the *Ludwigslied* and the "Muspilli," and a glossary). However, OHG is rather poor in texts reflecting any amount of the older way.

Gothic

Again, perhaps the most available learner's grammar is that of Wright, Joseph. *Grammar of the Gothic Language.* Oxford: Clarendon Press, 1954 (grammar, texts, glossary). Gothic and the Goths have acquired an extremely prestigious reputation over the centuries; however, the Go. texts which remain to us are essentially two in number, 1) a fragmentary translation of the Bible (by Bishop Wulfila [or Ulfilas]), and 2) a commentary on the Gospel of John. Gothic is invaluable to linguists, since outside of the early runic inscriptions, it is the oldest attested Germanic language (4th century CE).

In determining a course of action in the area of language-learning each student must balance all the factors of necessary sacrifice of time and effort, an honest appraisal of one's linguistic abilities, and the possible personal rewards growing out of one's efforts which will provide the necessary motivation.

REVIEWS

Review

Carlyle Pushong. *Rune Magic*. London: Regency, 1978.
(From *The Runestone*, Nr. 30, Winter 1979)

This little volume (100 pages) is quite valuable as an introduction to the modern runic tradition from an essentially eclectic point of view. It is a study by an outsider for outsiders. The basic philosophy behind the book is not compatible with the faith of Ásatrú, nor with the inner traditions of Runic Odinism. Some short quotes from the text may illustrate the non-Ásatrú approach to a subject which should, by our birth rights, belong to us. With respect to the relevance of "myth" Mr. Pushong states on page 19: "In a practical sense myths can not be revived ... myths can most certainly be looked upon with nostalgic sentiments of halcyon days perhaps paralleling the imaginative dreams of our childhood." This type of conception would seem to deny the eternal living essence of the myths and archetypes so vital to the ever-green nature of Ásatrú. On page 25, Mr. Pushong pens a most disturbing sentence: "Since there was no central religious authority or no recognized framework of doctrine, and since whatever doctrines were commonly accepted correlated closely at least in spirit with Christian beliefs and ceremonials, the transition to Christianity was easy and indeed painless."

Martyrs of Ásatrú, such as Raud the Strong, Eyvindr Kinnrifi, and Olvir would have a different version— let us hope Mr. Pushong never has to face their wrath! Much of the material in the book is lifted directly from German works by Karl Spiesberger. It is somewhat perturbing that this source is never acknowledged in footnotes or in the scanty bibliography. *Rune Magic* can be a valuable book, when read with the critical eyes of the Ásatrúarfólk.

Review

Þorsteinn Guðjónsson. *Astrobiology: The Science of the Universe*.
Reykjavík: Bioradii Publications, 1976.
(From *Rúna*, Vol. I, No. 2, Yule, 1982)

This work presents the revolutionary theories of the Icelandic scientist and philosopher Dr. Helgi Pjeturss (1872-1949), within the conception of the author— himself a leader of the "new Icelandic philosophy."

At the kernel of this new philosophy — this Nýall — is a revolutionary theory of sleep and dream, which to oversimplify, states that in dream we are actually perceiving an external reality being experienced at the same time by a "dream giver," who may be a being on this or some other planet. The process of transference is known as "bioinduction" (which is only one function of this phenomenon). Of course, a theory of this revolutionary nature must be studied in detail from the entire text of this book to receive justice.

The author is to a degree associated with the Ásatrú movement in Iceland, and although the work of the Nýall stands somewhat outside that of Ásatrú, it is nevertheless both historically and culturally associated with it, its philosophy compatible with that of Ásatrú. The work also offers an unusual opportunity for the reader of English to gain insight into the Icelandic intellectual, esoteric scene.

Review

Haack, Friedrichh-Wilhelm. *Wotans Wiederkehr: Blut-Boden-und-Rasse Religion*. Munich: Claudius Verlag, 1981.
(From *The Runestone*, No. 39, Spring 1982)

On the one hand this brand-new important study attempts to be a survey of the Neo-Germanic scene in Germany today. However, it also has a very definite purpose, i.e. to "warn" the good Christians of Germany about the rise of the old National Socialist specter in the cloak of Wôden. The author is himself a Lutheran pastor and teacher— and so his words must always be read with that in mind.

The Christian message is not a hidden one— it is openly stated. Haack's Christianity is rather of the social-justice-gospel type, and he seems most concerned with the rightist politics and racial ideologies lurking in these groups rather than their religious conceptions. The weakest aspect of the book is the author's practice of citing only those features which support his thesis. We would have hoped for a more objective representation of the overall philosophies of the organizations involved.

If all this is so, why is it even worth reviewing? The reasons are two: 1) it is nevertheless a fairly comprehensive view of a scene little known to most Ásatrúarfólk in Vinland, and 2) it has some invaluable suggestions and questions which should stimulate serious Ásatrú thinkers to deeper considerations of the faith and its destiny.

Haack spends too much space on groups which have little or nothing to do with Wotan— various Wagnerite Aryan-Christian groups ("Jesus was a German," etc.)— e.g. materialist-rationalist Ludendorff movement and Artgemeinschaft. In most cases he needs to do so to prove his racio-political thesis. However, in the case of the (now defunct) *Gylfiliten* he does not seem to have been forced to stretch the facts. The *Gylfiliten* in some instances had sunk into a regular form of Hitler-worship (!)— including "prayers" to him for the "unity of Germany."

The more positive groups, and ones more allied with us, e.g. the *Armanen Orden* (and *Guido-von-List-Gesellschaft*) under the Grand Masters Adolf and Sigrun Schleipfer and *Die Goden* ("the goðar"), pose more difficulties for the political nature of the author's work. These pages prove to be quite informative and interesting. Haack's greatest service to present day Ásatrú is, I think, his presentation of the well-known fact that most (if not all) of the racialist ideas sometimes present in Neo-Germanic "religious" movements have no foundation in ancient Germanic ideology but rather have their roots in the peculiar 19th century racial philosophy of J.A. Graf von Gobineau. Another constructive criticism forwarded by the author is that the Neo-Germanic ideologies tend to be based on emotionalism (emotive arguments) in which the controlling function of the rational mind has little input — in such a construct no "tradition of understanding" may be built up among the members — and so the groups inevitably sputter and/or split up.

For those who can read German, the work is well worth its price.

Review

Mund, Rudolf J. *Jörg Lanz von Liebenfels und der Neue Templer Orden: die Esoterik des Christentums.* Stuttgart: Rudolf Arnold Spieth Verlag, 1976.

(From *Rúna*, Vol. I, No. 2, Yule, 1982)

The Rune-Gild has a highly ambiguous interest in the subject of Lanz von Liebenfels (LvL). We are compelled to make a study of his work, 1) because it historically came in the period of the early 20th century GERMANIC Renaissance and was therefore deeply affected by it (and in turn it influenced the Renaissance itself?), and 2) because it has often been identified with this Germanic Rebirth by later investigators. Our task is to determine the true nature of this work and its possible relationship to the Germanic Renaissance (ca. 1880-1938)— this book by R. J. Mund proves to be a great aid in this undertaking.

Mund, who was a member of the Waffen SS and who is without doubt a writer sympathetic to the views of Lanz, presents a counter-study to that published in the 1950s by Dr. W. Daim, *Der Mann, der Hitler die Ideen gab* ("The Man who gave Hitler his Ideas"). Mund's scholarship in no way compares to Daim's, and sometimes the newer study strays off the track, for example into the history of the Templars (the supposed model for Lanz' Ordo Novi Templi— ONT). However, much of what Mund has to say is invaluable to a more balanced— and hence more correct— view of Lanz and his work.

The author supports his claim that Lanz never left the Cistercian *Heiligenkreuz Orden* (Order of the Holy Cross), nor the Christian Faith in spirit, and that he was not, as Daim maintains, ejected by the Order— by reporting (with impressive but inconclusive photographic evidence) that Lanz was in fact buried by the Holy Cross Brothers. Throughout, Mund emphasizes the fact that Lanz understood his work as being essentially Christian and that his racial doctrine was of a different type than understood by Daim, and even by later "admirers" of Lanz' work. Mund argues that the racial ideology of LvL was a "positive" one— one of self-development, Pan-Aryanism (which included Slavs), and tolerance for the rights of non-Aryans— all motivated by an essentially Christian viewpoint— and that his thoughts were usurped by the Nazis to their own political ends.

Lanz is considered by most to have been rabid anti-Semite (and he probably was by today's strict standards)— yet Mund points out that Lanz worked with Jews all his life (e.g. the collaboration with his long-time partner Rabbi Moriz Altschüller— who was also an official member of the board of directors of the Guido-von-List-Gesellschaft— on the *Monumenta Judaica*).

These, and other facts must give pause to those who would either damn Lanz as a "proto-Nazi," or use Lanz as an ideologue for their own brand of racist doctrine.

Mund goes too far in his assessment that because Lanz was not a Neo-Pagan, neither was Guido von List. While it is true that both were members of each other's organizations, any reading of the work of GvL must place him firmly in the (Neo-)Pagan camp, since his sacred models are the ancient Germanic culture, the Eddas, etc., while Lanz rarely used anything but the Judeo-Christian writings as models. This curious juxtaposition of Lanz and GvL is another aspect which needs further investigation.

Despite its scholarly shortcomings, the book is a must for those interested in the ONT and its founder.

Review

Hans F. Günter. *The Religious Attitudes of the Indo-Europeans.* tr. V. Bird. London: Clair Press, 1967.
(From *Rûna* vol. 1, no. 3 Midsummer, 1983)

The study of Indo-European roots — cultural, linguistic, as well as religious — can reveal much concerning the depth levels of our faith. However, this book does not afford us much of a view on these Indo-European roots as a whole. Its chief value is in its fundamentally Tiwic view of religion— an objectivist-rationalist view. What it has to say about Wôden is misguided in the extreme— especially from the Indo-European perspective. Günter ascribes any magico-shamanistic features to so-called "Hither-Asiatic" peoples and claims that true Indo-European religion was free of such things! At one point (p. 13) he says "The figure of Odin-Wodan does not belong to Indo-European religious history." Although this is not a new idea, Günter tries to take it further— into a modern value system.

The evidence that this is wrong is even partially presented by Günter himself. "Perhaps it is the name which is the unique feature of Odin that reaches back into Indo-European antiquity, for this root is derived from the Indo-European root *vat- meaning "to be spiritually excited", and as such it is still preserved in Sanskrit, in old Iranian and in Latin, where it corresponds to the word *vates*, meaning "a seer or a poet." (p. 12) But before going on, we must point out that this view (although still to be found in older handbooks, and so forth) is not the commonly held one today. The author makes several references to the French Indo-Europeanist Georges Dumézil— but seems to have entirely missed the main point of this scholar's work— that is, the original Indo-European religious structure consisted of a holistic complex of functions. All of these functions are present in all individual national systems in varying degrees of balance. To put it simply, the primal functional structure appeared:

    1st function: A. justice-law   B. magic-poetry   (Sovereignty)
    2nd function: war/defense   (Force)
    3rd function: fertility, wealth, eroticism   (Prosperity)

From this we can see that function IB (magic-poetry) was present from Proto-Indo-European days— and that a god (by some name) presided over it. The correspondence in name is less important than correspondence in function.

Only in function IA (justice-law) is there any nominal correspondence— Old Norse T‡r (PGmc. *Teiwaz), Greek Zeus, Latin Ju-pitar, and Sanskrit Dyauh. The functional correspondences from IB (magic-poetry) would be: Old Norse Óðinn, Greek Hermes, Latin Mercurius, Sanskrit Varuna. (For a summary of Dumézil's work, see C. Scott Littleton. *The New Comparative Mythology*. University of California Press, 1973.)

These patterns make it clear that a magico-poetic aspect was present in the Indo-European, and therefore in the ancient Germanic religion, from the beginning. Efforts to diminish this element often seem to be more on the order of philosophical projection/wish fulfillment than objective investigation.

If it is kept in mind that Günter is presenting a one-sided (uni-functional) picture of Indo-European religion, this can be used as a valuable work.

Review

Marijane Osborn and Stella Longland. *Rune Games*. Routledge & Keagan Paul, London, 1982.
(From *Rúna*, Vol. 1, No. 1, Ostara, 1983)

This welcome volume can lay clear claim to being the first book of serious runic mysticism to be published in English. It is quite obvious that a good deal of introspection and scholarship has gone into the preparation of the ideology and techniques outlined in the pages of this work although there are certain inexplicable scholarly errors, for example, on p. 16 the phrase "... the Hebrew alphabet, which is the only other Indo-European alphabet ...(!)".

But these can generally be ignored in favor of the useful methods of runic meditational divination detailed in the book. In all, some ten techniques or "games" — not frivolous but earnest play — based on the Old English Futhorc are outlined. A second feature of major importance is the stave-by-stave exploration of the runic cosmos— perhaps because the configuration of the Kabbalistic Tree of Life has become a modern occult dogma of sorts— the authors have chosen to attempt to fit the German World Tree, Yggdrasill, into the pattern of the Kabbalistic Tree. The result is unsatisfactory from both the runic and Kabbalistic viewpoint, I think. This is not to say the two systems can not be understood in terms of one another (to some extent at least)— but a scheme which places Midgard in Netzach and Hel in Malkuth seems rather problematic. It is unfortunate that Osborn and Longland did not use their obvious research abilities and speculative powers to find and develop the Yggdrasill configuration of the Nine Worlds. (A fuller account of this cosmological scheme has been published in *Runelore*.)

Another exemplary feature of this book is the art-work of Steven Longland which adds tremendous beauty and power to the text.

It is also worth quoting a passage, which might well be understood as an Ásatrú/Odinist thesis underlying the book. In the context of a discussion of the Tarot and the I-Ching, they write, "... 'The Rune Poem' contains in itself the best features of these two systems, while it has the further advantage that 'the runic cosmos' which it presents is closer to our own experience that the social structure of ancient China or the blend of Hebrew, medieval and pre-Raphaelite preoccupations evident in the various Tarot packs available... 'The Rune Poem' offers a fresh approach to the problems of individuality and existence that arises directly from the experience of the people of the northern latitudes." (pp. 22-23).

This book is destined to become a classic of rune-work and will be required reading for all Rune-Gild members.

Appendix A

The Awakening of a Runemaster
The Life of Edred Thorsson
by
James Allen Chisholm

Controversies and sensationalism seem to swirl about Edred Thorsson like the whirlwinds he has raised with his runic and Germanic studies. I suppose we should expect nothing other than this from a man and a magician who has dedicated himself to the way of Woden and to the work of expounding the Word *Rûna* ("sense of mystery") and thereby retrieve the soul of an entire folk. With this work comes the woe of often times being misunder-stood or misinterpreted by his contemporaries— so it has always been with such men. But if we in the Rune-Gild continually struggle to lift this curse by shedding ever more light on the runic teachings and lore pioneered in Edred's works. It is for this reason that the ways and circumstances under which Edred's thoughts evolved become relevant to the serious runic investigat-or. The story of Edred's life is not done— so no true "biography" is possible. All we can do here is outline the major developments in his life and ideas to sometime in the year 1996ev.

Edred was born on May 5, 1953 in a small north Texas town. He is the only child of Betty and Glendon Flowers, both native Texans. He had been conceived on August 20, the anniversary of the birthday of his dead grandfather after whom he was named. (This is also said by some to be the day, in 1953, when the fabled "Age of Aquarius" actually began.)

His mother was born Betty Jane Eden, daughter of Edred Cosgrove Eden (1888-1945) who is said to belong to the same house as Anthony Eden, Lord Avon. Of course, Edred never met his grandfather, who died before Edred was born. But mysterious-ly he felt the influence of this dead ancestor in his life. Edred's given surname, Flowers, is derived from Anglo-Saxon *flâer*, arrow-maker, and is a name common only in extreme southwestern England.

In his pre-school years Edred was able to spend a great deal of time with his father as well as his mother— and as an only child had their undivided attention. His father worked for the railroad, as his father had before him. In those early years Edred can remember that his father taught him the greatest of lessons: that in all things he could look to the depths of his own self, of his own heart, to a sense of what was right and wrong, that such a sense would never fail if it was used in a faithful way.

In 1960 his family moved to Dallas which he generally found depressing. Throughout his childhood and adolescence there he became progressively more introverted and caught up in worlds of his own making. He seemed to dwell in "a world of gods and monsters"— as Dr. Pretorius in one of his favorite films, *The Bride of Frankenstein* (1932) would say.

This introversion was suddenly — if only internally — broken in August of 1969 when he decided that upon graduation from high school he would go to Germany to seek adventure. This internal sense of adventure became a moment of great awakening. The next two years were spent in preparation for this event. Edred began to learn German— and began to think of a career in journalism.

In his senior year in high school he wrote an English paper on "The Truth and Superstition in Bram Stoker's *Dracula*." This was more than a year before the appearance of the McNally and Florescu book *In Search of Dracula*. The project was close to 50 pages in length— while the average student's paper was about one fourth that length. This was perhaps the first indication of Edred's ability to do research and treat topics with a broad scope of understanding. In doing research for this paper in 1970, he came across the world of the occult for the first time.

In September of 1971 Edred headed over the sea to Germany— having never before spent a night a way from some member of the family or close friend. The first 72 hours or so of this adventure taught the future explorer and creator of worlds and alternative universes great lessons. He knew he could travel outside his own small and narrow known world— and with the proper internal preparation — could pass into previously unknown spaces; and despite whatever fears and apprehensions he might have— he could flourish in these strange landscapes. When in Germany and central Europe, he had an uncanny feeling of being "at home."

His first two months in Germany were spent at the Goethe Institut in Prien am Chiemsee— the town giving access by ferry to the island of Herrenchiemsee on which king Ludwig II of Bavaria built one of his magnificent palaces. At the institute Edred made many good friends— some of whom were to provide strange adventures later. Some of these are too delicate to enter into in any detail here— but one is of special interest. Edred had always day-dreamed about being a "freedom fighter" on behalf of eastern European countries— at that time, 1971, still firmly in the grip of totalitarian communist regimes.

One of his friends, an expatriate of Hungary, gave Edred his chance— albeit a modest one. The person asked Edred to take certain messages and documents to an associate of his still in Hungary. There had originally been a band of seven friends who had sworn to escape from behind the Iron Curtain. All had escaped by one. Edred journeyed to Szekszard in central Hungary, delivered the messages and then stayed on for a couple of days. At this time this was a zone forbidden to foreigners, and soon his presence was discovered by the authorities. He was called in to the police headquarters, questioned and given until nightfall to get out of the country. He carried concealed replies to the original messages.

As the train sat on the border between Hungary and Austria, moments before departure into the west— Edred was removed from the train. As he walked to the guard station, he watched the train pull off into the darkness in the west. He was questioned by gun-toting goons for an hour. Luckily nothing was discovered, and nothing was revealed. Edred was escorted to the tracks where an engine crossed the border from the west to attach to a lone car in Hungary. Edred got on board and sat in the back of the car contemplating his good luck. After a few moments a gnome-like man dressed in the epitome of Austrian folk-costume appeared through the front of the car. Jovially he asked why Edred had been detained. Edred told him they thought he might be carrying some illegal documents, and assured the sympathetic "Austrian" that "they were mistaken." So the friendly man left by way of the door he had entered.

Just before the train departed, Edred saw the gnome leap from the train and duck into the guard-station. It was then that he began to understand that despite whatever *apparent* "power" a person or persons might believe themselves to have— most were in actuality somewhat below the mean of human potential.

Back in Germany, through contacts he made at the Institut, Edred became involved in the Sadean world of the Chateau Society (*Burggesellschaft*) and in the Order of the Triskelion (*Triskelenorden*). He was sworn to secrecy about these activities, which he could only speak about after 18 years had passed.

After several months of traveling around central Europe— with frequent "rest" periods at the "chateau" in a small mountain town near Prien, Edred returned to his parents' home in Dallas. One thing Edred fully realized was that the true thing, the right thing, for which he had set out to seek on his outward bound adventure, could only truly be found *inside* and must be sought first "at home."

Strangely — and all-too-humanly — Edred began to fall back into his old introverted behaviors back in his parental home. But internally he had changed forever. The tension between his internal urge to rebel against oppressive norms of society and the cosmos and the ordinary circumstances in which he was again living his life led him to seek out and join the by that time famous Church of Satan. This, he hoped, would help cause a similar breakthrough in his psyche that the trip to Germany had done. Edred still likes to tell how he finally decided to join the Church of Satan. He was taken to the largest Baptist church in San Antonio, Texas by his favorite aunt. There the good church-folk distributed a church magazine which featured the Church of Satan— ostensibly telling how "horrible" the Satanists were. The only trouble was, in this time before the church realized they had to lie and make up stories about what Satanists believed or did, the magazine simply told the truth about the thoughts of Anton LaVey— assuming these would be in and of themselves so outrageous as to outrage the good Bible-believing folk. But I was not outraged— I was fascinated and wanted to know, to experience, more of an unknown world.

Shortly after that he wrote to the Church of Satan and joined— unfortunately (?) the local representatives of the Church had just moved away from Dallas and so Edred had absolutely no contact with local Satanists— because there were no others. For the next year Edred was absorbed in practical and theoretical studies of the occult and Satanism. His chief source of inspiration was the *Cloven Hoof*, the periodical of the Church of Satan— then edited by Michael Aquino.

But because one of the chief reasons he became involved with the Church was to gain human associates from whom he might learn the secrets he sought, Edred's enthusiasm for the Church waned, as to him it was nothing but a paper organization.

From September of 1972 to May of 1973 Edred attended a community college in Dallas— there he liked to stir up the "Jesus Freaks" by parading around in full Satanic regalia— black and red clothing, pants tucked in high black boots, sporting a large "Baphomet" medallion (official sign of the Church of Satan). On numerous occasions the charismatic "Jesus Freaks" would try to cast out the demons obviously dwelling in Edred— an activity he very much enjoyed because it made him and his peculiar ways the center of attention. It even turned out to be a great gimmick for meeting girls!

One day, Edred was confronted by a man who, upon seeing his Satanic medallion said: "Ah... a Brother of the Left-Hand Path!" Edred began to talk to him, and from him learned of other traditions of magic— of the Kabbalah, the Golden Dawn, and of Aleister Crowley.

When the time came to renew membership in the Church of Satan, Edred simply did not do so— and thus his official career as a Satanist came to an end.

One of the chief influences — albeit indirect — that this teacher had on Edred was his introduction to the world of German occultism. Edred was directed to the book entitled *The Spear of Destiny* when it first came out in the United States in 1973, and further to the relevant sections of the *Morning of the Magicians*. The material in these works fascinated Edred— and suggested much more to him than they revealed.

In the summer of 1973 Edred moved to Austin, Texas to begin attending the University of Texas in the fall. During this summer he did volunteer work at the local occult bookstore/Liberal Catholic Church. There he not only became more familiar with the local occult world— but with the greater scope of occult and magical thought contained in the books in the store. He spent all his extra money — earned by chopping weeds for the city — on occult books of magic and mysticism.

During this time he came into contact with a group called the Nexalist Collegium, which was run by a Wiccan. The ostensible purpose of the group was to educate seekers on the theoretical level in various spiritual paths and then to guide them to ultimate active involvement in the school most compatible with their personal needs. This seemed a noble purpose.

It was at one of this group's Monday night open houses that Edred met Nancy. The relationship between them was to last 17 years. In the following year she was to become deeply involved in Wicca and it was through this indirect connection that Edred became familiar with the more inner workings of that system.

But for that year Edred continued to be involved with the theories and practices of ceremonial magic(k) and to explore an eclectic path generally of his own making. In this period Edred was prevented from giving much credence to the Wiccan forms of "magic"— because as a system it emphasized — derived from its essentially *religious* worldview — a harmonizing of the will of the individual with the patterns of nature. Edred had made the essentially *magical* and individualistic philosophy he originally found earlier too much a part of himself to allow this.

During the summer of 1974 Edred and his then wife were persuaded by a rather zany member of the Wiccan coven — actually its "high priestess" — to go down near Houston to the home of a magician then using a Tibetan stage name. Some months before they had all witnessed his act of stage magic dressed up to look like Tibetan miracle working. The high priestess just knew she was in psychic contact with the lama through dreams and was sure she would be welcomed with open arms when she arrived on his doorstep. When they pulled up to his run-down ranch style house in the middle of an oil field with broken down sports cars all around it— Edred says at this point he began to get the feeling he'd been "had" on some level. The priestess rang the doorbell and the rinpoche came to the door- he was a far cry from the way he looked on stage at the psychic fair in Dallas. Now he was in blue jeans, a too-small T-shirt and he had a brewski in his hand— an occultnik icon for the masses to be sure. The most venerable lama sent the group packing with little explanation— the trip back to Austin was said to have been a quiet one.

In the still boredom of the return trip, Edred says he heard a voice— audibly pronounce the sound "roonah." He understood enough immediately to know that this had *something* to do with the "runes"— the old pre-Christian writing system used by the Germanic peoples. So the next day he went to the University of Texas library, then located in the infamous tower from which Charles Whitman rained death in the summer of 1966, and checked out all sorts of books on runes and runic writing. Among these, quite oddly, was *Runenmagie* by Karl Spiesberger (1955). It is really a minor miracle that such an out and out occult book would be found in an academic library such as the one at the university.

Edred began at once to study the Spiesberger book and put the magic in it to practical use. During the summer of 1975 he did many daily workings, called "Mead-Rites," in a special chamber dedicated exclusively to do this work. The purpose of these workings was to spread the might of the runes over the world and to give him the inspiration and wisdom necessary to this work. At the same time Edred composed a complete manuscript of rune magic in the *Armanen* system. This was originally entitled *A Primer of Runic Magic*— but has to date never been published. Although several major publishers were interested in it at the time all ultimately rejected it because they thought "runes wouldn't sell."

This apparent set-back was subsequently interpreted as "the hand of Woden." Of course, the 18-rune Armanic Futhork is a pseudo-runic system and despite whatever inspiration, wisdom and power Edred may have gained from it in those early months, it soon became clear that his work was to be the restoration of the traditional and authentic system of the 24 runes.

In the years 1976-1979 Edred dedicated himself to reconstructing authentic runic traditions and Germanic cultural and religious concepts. He began his studies of ancient and modern Germanic dialects at the University of Texas— Old Norse, Middle High German, and modern Scandinavian languages. His special academic field in this period was Old Norse and the study of ancient Germanic concepts of the soul and the cosmos. He felt that to understand the basis of the ancient ways, one would have to get into the souls of the ancients as deeply as possible. it was also during this period that he became aware of neo-Germanic religious organizations such as the Ásatrú Free Assembly and the Odinist Fellowship.

In May of 1979, Edred received an M.A. degree with a thesis entitled *Rebirth and Rites of Transformation in the Saga of Sigurðr Sigmundarson*. (This was later released on a limited basis within the Rune-Gild under the title *Sigur›r, Rebirth and Initiation*.) The very next month he finished the manuscript for *Futhark: A Handbook of Rune Magic*, which was a 24-rune based revision of his earlier manuscript on rune magic. His private runic studies and course of early development which had begun in 1974 had been competed.

Also in 1979 Edred founded the Austin "*skeppslag,*" later called "kindred," of the AFA and began local organizational work. In the course of this work Mitchell Edwin Wade made contact with Edred and soon became his chief associate.

Near Midsummer 1980, Edred, along with his trusted stalwart Edwin Wade, attended the First Althing of the AFA near Lafayette, California. At this time he was also formally and ritually installed by Stephen McNallen as a *goði*, or priest, in the AFA. During the years between 1979 and 1981 Edred, along with Edwin, built up the kindred on a spiritual level. Edred wrote a full set of seasonal blessings and performed them during these years. The ceremonies were based on the best scholarly research available. Many of these were eventually published some ten years later in *A Book of Troth*.

From his entry into the AFA in 1978 (he carried AFA membership card #072) to the eventual demise of that organization in 1987, Edred remained of the opinion that the AFA was *the* religious organization to represent the interests of the common Elder Troth in North America. This was basically due to the nature of the implicit heroic vision of the AFA— the reestablishment of the Elder Troth among its folk. As the reprinted articles in this volume show, Edred was a regular contributor to *The Runestone*, the journal of the AFA.

With the maturing of Edred's runic studies, both academic and magical, he was guided to found the Rune-Gild during the Yule-Tide of 1979/1980. The Gild was to undergo many transformations over the next several years as it grew with its founder. However, it was then, and it remains today, the only truly *initiatory* runic organization in the world based on the actual traditions of the ancient Germanic peoples. The body of teachings which would eventually emerge as books such as *Runelore* and *The Nine Doors of Midgard* were already taking definite shape at this time.

In the meantime his graduate-level work continued in the field of Medieval Studies. All in all, Edred considers his whole career in Graduate School at the University of Texas as a seminary for the true priesthood of the Germanic tradition. He used his over ten years of academic training as a time of preparation for his later, more public, activity.

Edred spent the latter part of 1981 and the first half of 1982 studying academic runology in Göttingen, Germany under the preeminent runologist Klaus Düwel. These and other researches emerged in his 1984 dissertation entitled *Runes and Magic*. (This was subsequently published by Peter Lang Verlag in 1986.)

Also during this "German period" Edred became associated with the *Armanen Orden* and attended their gatherings in an ancient castle in central Germany. He was, however, never formally or ritually initiated in any of their rites. Many other contacts were made and seeds of future work planted during this time— most of which he began to cultivate and publish throughout the 1980s. Contact was again made with the *Burggesellschaft*.

Edred travelled widely visiting Iceland, the British Isles, Scandinavia and various places on the Continent. Special "pilgrimages" were made to the Þingvellir in Iceland, Gamla Uppsala in Sweden, and the *Externsteine* in northern Germany and to the native region of his soul— southwestern England (Wessex).

The subsequent two years were spent finishing his dissertation. In 1984 he received his doctorate in Germanic Studies and began his career as a university lecturer.

During those two years he began to have some doubts about the future of the AFA as the institution that could fulfill the mission of reestablishing the troth of his ancestors. But he played no part in the eventual demise of the AFA— nor was he asked to help in its reorganization. As he sees the AFA situation now, it essentially failed because its leadership consistently sacrificed principles to expediency— with little advantage gained from the effort.

At the same time, on an intellectual level Edred was growing more and more uneasy with ideas concerning the exclusively pantheistic and naturalistic tendencies present in the average neo-pagan, neo-Germanic groups. These notions did not quite fit comfortably with what he had learned in academic circles concerning the often abstract and sophisticated levels of thought inherent in the Germanic ideology. The idea that the gods and goddesses were simply personifications of "natural forces," or that they were deifications of prehistoric personages, were seen clearly in the light of the history of mythological studies as merely reflections of earlier, less refined (and less accurate) stages of modern understanding.

Independently Edred began to experiment with darker forces, and briefly founded an organization called the Order of the Shining Trapezoid. Workings connected with this and the Odian stream made it clear to him that there was another branch of the Odian stream with which he was not yet familiar— and he began to seek this out.

It was shortly after this time that Edred was re-introduced to an old, yet at that time unknown, mentor— Dr. Michael A. Aquino. As it turns out, many of the *Cloven Hoof* articles which had influenced Edred early on were written anonymously by Aquino who was then editor of that journal. Edred learned that Michael Aquino had formed the Temple of Set in 1975 in an effort to maintain the legitimate aspects of the Church of Satan, which he saw as being betrayed by Anton LaVey. The Temple of Set had developed an entire special interest focus more or less in the field of Germanic magic and had reconstructed the Order of the Trapezoid as an expression of this. Edred saw this as another Gate to Valhalla and became a member of the Temple of Set in early February 1984. He was quickly recognized to the second degree of Adept and to the Priesthood (III°) on October 7, 1984. It would be a mistake to assume that Edred was merely being recognized for his previous accomplishments. The philosophical sophistication and magical precision expressed in the work of Michael Aquino (principally through the fundamental Temple document "Black Magic") made clear what had only been murky before.

To transform Runic magic and the new Germanic tradition in any *real* way, Edred found that he must be able to step *outside* of its organic structure. In order to heal and retrieve the soul of the Germanic tradition, he would, like Óðinn, have to storm the Gates of Hel— to go outside of the accepted bounds of order. He knew at the time that he would be little appreciated for his efforts— thus it is often the fate of heroes that they begin their lives as villains. However, he trusted, and trusts even now, that he was following his wyrd and not striving against it, when he entered upon the "Dark Road."

In the five years between 1985 and 1990 Edred completed no less than nine manuscripts for publication— almost all of them involved with the ancient Germanic tradition. this was a period of intense intellectual and magical work. On November 14, 1986 he was recognized as a Magister Templi (IV°) within the Temple of Set. Subsequent to this he began to understand the pivotal subjective event of the summer of 1974 in a clearer light. As exposure to the Temple philosophy had clarified his relationship to the Germanic tradition, so it had eventually illuminated his relationship to himSelf and to Woden. The *true character* of his Work became clear.

Edred was not only to understand the Runes, but to activate and focus them that they could have a direct effect on the world— in a way more widespread than they had ever had in their ancient manifestation.

One of the side benefits, as Edred apparently sees it now, of his association with the darker cycles of esotericism is that it brings the Odian current of today into closer harmony with its perceived nature in ancient times. The god Óðinn had in elder times a reputation for dark and inscrutable dealings. Many, if not most, involved in "modern" Ásatrú or Odinism had in their minds "converted" Odin into a benign father-figure or worse yet into a mere symbol of Germanic nationalism. The dark and mysterious (= Runic) aspect — which is the essence of that Óðinn is all about — seemed virtually lacking. Descending with Óðinn into the darker cycles was seen by Edred as *a* way to recover the awe-inspiring aspect of the true Odian soul.

All in all, the years between 1985 and 1990 proved to be highly productive. For every project finished there were three or four conceived and begun on some level. However, it was also a period of some personal disillusionment. Edred had written his dissertation at a major university (the University of Texas, Austin) in a classic field of Germanic philology— runology. The contents were being accepted (and continue to be accepted) by runologists around the world as the most convincing scholarly treatment of the magical component in the runic tradition. Yet no university department would hire him. His feelings on this are ultimately mixed. Because he was not drawn into the often petty and intellectually dishonest world of academia he has remained free to pursue his studies on a more pure and personal basis. At the same time he sees the reluctance of departments to hire him as an expression of their essential and growing opposition to the study of ancient European traditions— especially the *vital* ones. What departments often seemed to want were such things as experts in East German "culture and literature"— how quickly they can be made to be irrelevant! Sometimes Edred would be told by would-be "employers" that his dissertation topic "runes and magic" was just "too far out" — too much outside the mainstream — this sentiment most often coming from tenured professors with dissertations entitled things such as "The Theory of Voice in the Early Verses of Hölderlin"... All in all, however, Edred seems to have seen the guiding hand of the All-Father in this aspect of his life— there are hundreds of professors of Germanic studies in the world today ... but only *one* Edred Thorsson.

In late November of 1987 the AFA collapsed and its leader headed for the hills. This caught Edred rather by surprise, it seems. He had shown no previous interest in establishing or leading a *religious* organization in Ásatrú/Odinism. But he knew that such an organization was to be of greatest importance to the over all health and well-being of the greater Neo-Germanic movement. He perceived that the "Raven Banner," a magical symbol for the struggle to reestablish the Elder Troth, had been allowed to fall by demise of the AFA, and he instantly knew that it had fallen to him to raise it back up. But since the Elder Troth was a *folk movement*, anything meant to represent that stream of thought would also have to be such a movement. When an organization belonged to "one man," as the AFA had, it could be destroyed by one man.

It therefore came to pass that on Mother Night, December 20, 1987, Edred led a magical Working for the hallowing of the Ring of Troth. In this Working a magical link was formed with the All-Father and with the whole of the Great Tradition. The leadership of the organization of the Ring itself first fell to me, James A. Chisholm. Although Edred had little or nothing to do with the day-to-day operations of the Ring of Troth, he remained a sort of spiritual advisor, and was the original "architect" of the Ring.

During the year of 1989 certain individuals began a hate campaign against Edred. By taking advantage of the Fundamentalist Christian / Therapeutic State atmosphere of the country during the late 1980s these few individuals "accused" Edred of involvement in "diabolical things." Edred had never made a secret of his involvement in the Temple of Set— but these apparent agents for the Christian Right thought it made a better story to act as if he had. The motives of these people can only be guessed at from their own personal backgrounds, characters and eventual fates. It was widely assumed that Edred would have raised a niding-pole against the chief instigator of this hate campaign— he did not. But I cursed him that the world would know of his treacherous nature. Edred's only "curse" was to send the message to Valhalla: "Let the Will of Woden be done in this thing!" This individual is now quite insane— doing hard time in a Texas prison for the murder of his own wife...

By 1990 the elements were in place for a great personal transformation. The Rune-Gild had passed through its embryonic state and was emerging as the true initiatory body it had always been intended to be. (The final fruition of this embryonic state was the publication of *The Nine Doors of Midgard* in May of 1991.) On a more personal level, however, it was a major event in the summer of 1990 — Edred's recognition to the Fifth Degree in the Temple of Set which served as a catalyst for enormous change.

Life — both internal and external — as well as the world around him — had to be transformed according to the ideals implicit in his Fifth Degree Word: RÛNA. Things that had remained hidden within him now cried out for manifestation both in the inner and outer worlds.

In the twilight of 1990 Edred met another catalyst in his life. It is known that it is quite common for true Magi — those whose philosophies have been crystallized into a single Word from which, and according to which, the whole philosophy is expressed— to have great need of a female consort and companion who by their very *natures* embody the essence of the Word. Simon Magus had his Helene, Jesus his Magdelene— Crowley sought but perhaps never recognized his true "Whore of Babylon." But to all true Magi such are delivered by force of Necessity— and once provided they must be recognized and an eternal bond with them established. Such was Edred's response to Crystal Dawn who proved to provide the key to his heart, to his life and to his Word and Work.

It was also at this time that the 18-year ban on the manifestation of the Order of the Triskelion was lifted. This organization for the practice of operant Sadeanism and Carnal Alchemy was founded in early 1991 by Edred and Crystal Dawn.

Most of the year 1991 was spent in a semi-haunted old house on Manor Road in one of Austin, Texas' most degenerate neighborhoods. It was in this house that some radical magical experiments were undertaken. I know about these because we shared that house, and I was privy to many of the experiments.

At the Ostara gathering of the Ring of Troth in March of 1992, the reigns of administrative power were handed over to Prudence Priest and a full contingency of Rede members by me— which brought the stormy first phase of the history of the Ring of Troth to an end.

From then on Edred was able to spend most of his energies on matters pertaining to the Rune-Gild.

1993 marked a transitional year in Edred's development. It is the end of one nine-year cycle and the beginning of another. The great project of actually creating an alternative universe in the wilderness east of Austin was set into motion when Edred and Crystal bought 30 acres of forested land adjacent to Buescher State Park. It is on this land that the future history of the Gild and of Edred's many other undertakings will be written.

By the end of 1993 Edred and Crystal had moved to Woodharrow and over the next two years they built up the physical facilities on the land. A meeting hall was erected, and with the help of their many friends in Texas the work of finishing it was complete by the beginning of 1996. The publishing company they formally began in 1993, Rûna-Raven Press, has continued to develop over the years.

Due to inner turmoil in the Ring of Troth, Edred withdrew from any involvement with that organization at the Spring Equinox (Easter) of 1995. In August of that same year Crystal and Edred made a trip to Iceland and England in order to strengthen the work of the Gild in England and to make contact with the *landvættir* once more in order that the work of the Gild might be renewed.

In April of 1996 Edred retired from his position as Grand Master of the Order of the Trapezoid in order to focus more intently on Rune-Gild matters.

It is clear than in many ways this may be an untimely moment to write a study of the life of Edred Thorsson— for it seems that this is but the beginning of his true life as he was born to live it. The future will hold many more mysteries than has the past— but as yet that saw remains to be told.

Appendix B

Introductory Information
The Outer Hall of the Rune-Gild

Runes are the mysteries that underlie all of the worlds— that which lies *hidden* in, and gives power to, all things. These runes pull those who seek them ever onward and upward. Knowledge of them and the quest for their mastery within the self and throughout the worlds is the path of Odianism, or Rune-Wodenism. This quest leads to transformation— in the Self and in the Worlds.

As a practical matter, the Odian path has, until recently, been obstructed by a general lack of available information on a refined and authentic level. The Rune-Gild has undertaken to remedy this lamentable situation. But beyond this goal, our intention is to provide a gateway into the practical application of runic principles. It is imperative that a number of individuals be initiated into the intellectual and working aspects of runology. The soul of our folk has little chance of survival — much less of being as great as it is destined to become — if it is not armed with the Secrets of the Self. These secrets are the runes.

Because knowledge of the runes has languished under suppression in the distant past, and under ill-conceived superficial studies in the more recent past, it is now necessary that seekers along the true rune-roads gain deep and sound intellectual knowledge along with more practical work in runecraft. Knowledge and Work must always go hand in hand.

History of the Gild

The Rune-Gild was founded in 1980 as the first authentic rebirth of the elder runic tradition to the available to the new Gild siblings in about a thousand years. Over the ensuing years, the Gild has grown and changed its form as new information and impulses entered into its knowledge base, and as its leadership became more initiated. However, our aim has remained true and steadfast— to see the ancient gild of runemasters again make their wisdom known and felt in the world of their descendants. This is a great task, for those interested in the heritage of the Germanic or Teutonic peoples— and this should include all those who live in countries in which a Germanic language (e.g. English) predomin-ates — it may indeed be the greatest task that lies before us. For without the deep level spiritual heritage to guide us we will surely be lost in a morass of cultural confusion. The runes stand ready, the Runemasters and Drightens know their duty, but each sibling must work for his or her own initiation. The doors of the Gild Hall now stand open— enter with heart, enter with mind — and learn again the ways of the elder runemasters, and learn the ways of the new runemasters.

With the publication of *Futhark: A Handbook of Rune Magic*, *Runelore: A Handbook of Esoteric Runology*, and *At the Well of Wyrd: A Handbook of Runic Divination* the gates were opened. The time has now come to have those of you who will, enter the first doors of a graded approach to rune-work and rune-craft. In the Rune-Gild you will be introduced to a graded series of exercises known as the *Nine Doors of Midgard*. In these exercises you will learn various techniques of rune-work: more explicitly of rune-thinking (meditation/contemplation), rune-casting (divination), galdor (incantational or verbal magic), making of rune-tines (talismans) and other forms of rune-craft (operative magic) and rune-work (self-transformational activity), as well as many other techniques that were only touched on in a cursory fashion in *Futhark* and *At the Well of Wyrd*. The first three books by Thorsson were the beginning— the Rune-Gild itself is a road which is an end in and of itself.

The curriculum of the Gild is based on the oldest and most traditional runology of the Erulians. From this traditional base— which, as you probably know, all profane approaches to the runes recently published lack— the sibling (member) will be guided to levels of knowledge completely unavailable through other avenues.

Structure of the Rune-Gild

In the Gild there are three levels or "degrees" of initiation. These are based on the most ancient steps of learning any skill known in the elder age— that of apprentice, journeyman, and master. In the terminology of the Gild, however, these are reflected in the names or titles Learner, Fellow, and Runemaster. The Work of the Learner is made up of the *Nine Doors of Midgard*.

The Gild is divided into Inner and Outer Halls. The Outer Hall of the Gild is made up of those who are now working on the curriculum of the *Nine Doors of Midgard* and who want to be in close contact with the Gild and its magical Hall-Workings. But if there is a Runemaster or Hall-Leader in your area who is running a Gild-Hall, there will also most likely be Outer Hall Workings and gatherings which you could attend. Also, members are encouraged to set up Runa-Workshops ("runic study groups") in geographical areas where no Hall exists. Most siblings in the Outer Hall will be working alone, or in Runa-Workshops. It can not be said too often that the Gild does not deal in "mail-order occultism." For entry into the Inner Hall can only be gained in person and through personal contact with a Runemaster of the Gild.

The Inner Hall is made up of Fellows and Runemasters who have completed the *Nine Doors of Midgard* curriculum, or its equivalent, and who have been *personally* inducted by a Gild-Drighten.

In the Outer Hall the Gild is quite loose in its formal organization— it is rather like an extended magical study group. The practical advantages to actual membership in the Outer Hall are the extensive personal contacts that can be made, information on all the latest developments in the world of rune magic, and most importantly the inner magical keys to making the Hall-Workings true *magical links* between yourself and the Gild-Halls (both Inner and Outer) around the world.

A final word might be mentioned on the Gild-Drightens. They are a distinguished group of individuals each with their own area of expertise, each with their own unique gifts to offer the Gild. The Yrmin-Drighten, Edred Thorsson, is the author of the three books *Futhark*, *Runelore*, and *At the Well of Wyrd* (all published by Samuel Weiser) which are the three major "textbooks" of Rune-Gild work. He also holds a Ph.D. in Germanic Studies from a major university. Many of the other Drightens are similarly qualified.

Goals of the Gild

Among the most important goals of the Gild are the continued development of traditional and transformational runelore and the dissemination of that system to those who are inspired by the quest for the runes. We continue to institute runic study groups or Rûna-Workshops around the world. In addition to this, there is an ever expanding network of Inner Gild Halls open to siblings who are personally invited by a local Runemaster to join a Gild-Hall.

It can not be overemphasized that the main work of the Gild is centered in each individual, and its main aim is the self-transformation of each sibling according to the ancient principles of Odianism. For it is only from this basis of transformed individuals that the new Gild can be reborn in the full essence of the elder Gild of the Erulians.

For such transformations to occur there come key moments in the individual development of each Runer when *personal* contact with a true Rune-Master is Needed. The Rune-path may begin in solitude, and may end there, but in the middle there comes a time to interact with those who bear the Flame and who can show it to you.

To this end the foundation of the first permanent Hall of the Gild — the Yrmin-Hall — was laid in late 1993 and it was fully erected in the early part of 1994. It is situated on 30 acres of land near Austin, Texas. The estate is known as *Woodharrow*. It is here that Gild-Moots and seminars in advanced Rune-Work are held. It is to this Hall that Gilders of the future will come, be transformed, and go forth to spread the Word, which is *Rûna*.

The Work of the Gild can be summed up in the Seed-Word *Rûna* — "The Mystery," especially as extended and articulated through the stave: *Reyn til Rûna*— "Seek toward the Mysteries!" *Rûna* is the Hidden in the World, and the Sense of the Hidden lying within the depths of the Self. This eternal Quest is the essence of Rune-Work— and its fulfillment is the highest goal of the Gild.

If you choose to seek sponsorship for affiliation with the Gild, fill out the enclosed application form (including the attached questions) and send it in along with your Gild-toll. (The toll will be refunded if for any reason you cannot be sponsored.) For your first year's toll you will receive in your initial package all of the publications that were put out that year. Acceptance of your toll makes you a member of the Gild, which will be certified with a letter from the Yrmin-Drighten. You will also receive four issues of the Yrmin-Drighten's personal communique *Rune-Kevels*, which will keep you up to date on all events and publications of the Gild from around the world in the area of Rune-Galdor. *Rune-Kevels* is available to Gilders only. However, the most important document that you will receive is the *Gildisbók,*, which is an approximately 200-page book-length guide to the inner teachings of the Gild. It contains otherwise unpublished material on the history of the Gild, its cosmological and initiatory teachings and many other aspects of Rune-Lore and Rune-Work divided into nine main chapters or sections supple-mented by several appendices. The *Gildisbók*, like *Rune-Kevels*, is strictly reserved to Gild members only.

The Doors of Valhalla stand wide open— but it is now your task to step forth through the Doors of Midgard to face the challenges of a new way of being that awaits you within. The Gild stands ready to help you in this work— as no other organization in the world today can do. We welcome those who now wish to join us in the runic quest!

Appendix C

Information on the Rune-Gild Valid after Midsummer 1990
On Entry into the Rune-Gild

Thank you for your inquiry into the Rune-Gild. Over the past ten years we have had thousands of inquiries— and hundreds have joined the Gild. A new phase is now being entered into.

As of Midsummer (June 21) 1990 the Rune-Gild was closed to all **unsponsored** *members.*

This new policy has been put into place because the Gild will now be growing on a more local level. This means more involvement of the local Stewards of the Gild.

If you have recently written for information to the Gild you should read below to find out how you might gain entry into the Gild in the future. Your name and address will probably be sent to a local Steward, who may contact you for a more personal exchange.

How to Gain Sponsorship

To be sponsored you might get a recognized leader of the Gild (a Steward, Hall-Leader, Runemaster, or Drighten) to speak for you, and to sign the application form stating that they indeed do speak for you. The only way to get such sponsorship is really to give the Steward or Runemaster some indication of your level of runic initiation. Only those who have undertaken some form of self-study and self-initiation in the runes will generally be sponsored for membership in the Gild. The inquiries of those who write for information on the Gild will usually be forwarded to a local leader who may act on it further. Inquiries which demonstrate high levels of merit will be acted on directly by the Yrmin-Drighten, and will be sponsored for membership. *Sponsorship is gained only through a demonstration of a certain level of Runic initiation.* At present the easiest way to gain sponsorship is to write to the Yrmin-Hall and request an **Application for Sponsorship**— which consists of answering several questions. Those whose applications for sponsorship are accepted will be sponsored into the Gild by the Yrmin-Drighten, or Gild-Steward.

How to Gain First Runic Initiation

The first step in gaining true runic initiation is to begin the Rune-Gild course of study called *The Nine Doors of Midgard*. Experience has shown, however, that since the true runic stream was again unleashed in the world in the mid-1970s, there have been a number of brave souls who have won their way into Runic initiation. But these make themselves obvious upon first contact with the Gild. The leadership of the Gild can recognize true Rune-knowledge and Rune-skill when we see and hear it. If you have such knowledge, you must *communicate* it to the leadership before such can be recognized.

If you are seeking the beginnings of Rune-wisdom, you should undertake the road of self-initiation according to the traditional methods outlined in *The Nine Doors Of Midgard*. After you have gained a certain level of initiation — your inner Runic sense will tell you when — you should contact the Gild with your will to enter into our Halls. In doing this you must communicate what you believe to be the *essence* of your Runic initiation— and in some fashion demonstrate your level of Rune-knowledge. At that point you may be sponsored "at large" by a leader of the Gild. For the most part, however, the Gild seeks to get away from the structure of "mail order initiation." This stage has been to some extent necessary during the first ten years of the Gild's existence. But things are changing now. The training program of *The Nine Doors* is now available. There are local Stewards and Runemasters all over the world now. There may not be one in every community— but that is our ultimate goal. This can not be done by "mail order" though.

The first steps in true Runic initiation are contained in the traditional body of Rune-Lore outlined most completely in *The Nine Doors Of Midgard*.

Several years ago there was nothing to guide the aspiring Rune-worker. Now there is a whole corpus of literature and teachings. Unfortunately there is a great deal of chaff among the wheat grains of true lore— but that was put there for a purpose as well. Part of the process of true Runic initiation is learning to separate the wheat from the chaff. This whole body of true Runic material is your first field of working— explore it, learn from it, put its ways into action. Then you will be prepared for entry into the Gild itself.

The Rune-Gild is and always has been the true repository of Rune-knowledge. It is actually a remanifestation of the ancient gild of Rune-masters. It remains guided by the true Erulians. But to gain entry you must work your way from the beginning.

Information printed in Appendices B and C are for historical purposes only. For current entry policies and a description of the Rune-Gild as is currently configured, go to www.rune-gild.org.

Glossary

This glossary of technical words used in many of the articles found in this book indicates the exact intended definitions of words that might be used in unfamiliar contexts. The Old English or Old Norse terms from which some of these technical terms are ultimately derived are also provided.

Alsherjargoði: The common or "high" priest of a particular Ásatrú organization.
Æsir, sg. Áss : The gods and goddesses of consciousness in the Teutonic pantheon, governing the powers of sovereignty and physical force.
Asgard: The enclosure of the gods, the realm where the gods and goddesses exist. (ON *Ásgarðr*)
etin: A "giant," which is a living entity of great age, strength, and often knowledge. (ON *jötunn; jötnar*)
folk: 1) The Teutonic or Germanic nation (all people of Teutonic heritage, German, English, Dutch, Scandinavian, etc.), 2) The people gathered for a holy event.
holy: There are two aspects to this term: 1) that which is filled with divine power, and 2) that which is marked off and separate from the profane.
hugr: The cognitive part of the soul, the intellect or "mind." Also called hidge.
hamr: The quasi-physical part of the soul which gives a person shape and form.
lore: The tradition in all its aspects.
Midgard: the dwelling place of humanity, the physical plane of existence. Also, Mid-yard, the enclosure in the midst of all. (OE *Middangeard*)
multiverse: The totality of the "universe" seen not as a unit but as a compilation of graduated or segmental worlds. This term is opposed to the idea of *universalism*, i.e. that there is one *standard of reality*.
rede: Council or advice.
soul: 1) A general term for the psychic parts of the psycho-physical complex, 2) The postmortem shade. (OE *sâwl*)
sumble: The sacred ritual feast at which boasts are drunk. (OE *symble*, ON *symbl*)
troth: Religion, being loyal to the gods and goddesses and cultural values of the ancestors. (OE *trêofl*, ON *trú*)
true: Adjectival form of "troth," can mean "loyal." A "true man" is a man loyal to the gods and goddesses of his ancestors.
Vanir sg. Van: The gods and goddesses of organic existence in the Teutonic pantheon, governing the realms of organic production, eroticism, wealth, craftsmanship, and physical well-being.
wight: A being or entity of any kind with some living quality.
óðr: An emotive, synthesizing part of the soul which brings various aspects together in a powerful and inspired way. (OE *wôd*)
world: The psycho-chronic human aspects of the manifested universe. (OE *weoruld*, the age of a man.) The cosmos.
wyrd: The process of the unseen web of synchronicity and cause and effect throughout the cosmos. Same as weird.

Bibliography

Adler, Margot. *Drawing Down the Moon.* New York: Viking, 1979. (2nd ed. 1986.)
Agrell, Sigurd. *Die pergamenische Zauberscheibe und das Tarockspiel.* (= Humanistiska vetenskapssanfundet i Lund Årberattelse 1935-36) Lund, 1935-36.
Aswynn, Freya. *Leaves of Yggdrasil.* St. Paul, MN: Llewellyn, 1990.
Auld, Richard L. "The Psychological and Mythic Unity of the God Odhinn." *Numen,* 23:2 (1976), 145-160.
Baetke, Walter. *Das Heilige im Germanischen.* Tübingen: Mohr, 1942.
Bauschatz, Paul C. "The Germanic Ritual Feast." In: *The Nordic Languages and Modern Linguistics 3,* Ed. John M. Weinstock. Austin: University of Texas Press, 1976.
—————————. *The Well and the Tree: World and Time in Early Germanic Culture.* Amherst: University of Massachusetts Press, 1982.
Benveniste, Emile. *Indo-European Language and Society.* tr. E. Palmer. Coral Gables, FL: University of Miami Press, 1973.
Campbell, Joseph. *The Hero with a Thousand Faces.* (= Bollingen Series 17) Princeton: Princeton University Press, 1949.
Chaney, William A. *The Cult of Kingship in Anglo-Saxon England.* Berkeley: University of California Press, 1970.
D'Ardenne, S.R.T.O. "A Neglected Manuscript of British History." In: *English and Medieval Studies,* eds. Norman Davis and C. L. Wrenn. London: George Allen & Unwin, 1962, pp. 84-93
Davidson, Hilda R. (Ellis). *The Road to Hel.* Cambridge: Cambridge University Press, 1943.
Davidson, H.R. Ellis. *Gods and Myths of Northern Europe.* Harmondsworth: Penguin, 1964.
—————————. *Pagan Scandinavia.* New York: Praeger, 1967.
—————————. *Myths and Symbols in Pagan Europe.* Syracuse, NY: Syracuse University Press, 1988.
Dumézil, Georges. *The Destiny of a Warrior.* tr. A. Hiltebeitel. Chicago: University of Chicago Press, 1970.
—————————. *From Myth to Fiction: The Saga of Hadingus.* tr. D. Coltman. Chicago: University of Chicago Press, 1973.
—————————. *Gods of the Ancient Northmen.* E. Haugen, ed. Berkeley: University of California Press, 1973.
Eckhardt, Karl August. *Irdische Unsterblichkeit: Germanischer Glaube an die Wiederverkörperung in der Sippe.* Weimar: Bohlaus, 1937.
Eliade, Mircea. *The Myth of the Eternal Return or Cosmos and History.* (=Bollingen Series 46) tr. W. Trask. Princeton: Princeton University Press, 1971 [1954].
—————————. *Rites and Symbols of Initiation.* tr. W. Trask. New York: Harper and Row, 1958. (Also published as *Birth and Rebirth.*)
—————————. *Yoga: Immortality and Freedom.* (=Bollingen Series 56) tr. W. Trask. Princeton: Princeton University Press, 1958.
—————————. *Shamanism: Archaic Techniques of Ecstasy.* (=Bollingen Series 76) tr. W. Trask. Princeton: Princeton University Press, 1964.
—————————. *A History of Religious Ideas.* tr. W. Trask. Chicago: University of Chicago Press, 1978-1985, 3 vols.
Elliott, Ralph. *Runes: An Introduction.* Manchester: Manchester University Press, 1959.
Finch, R. G. *The Saga of the Volsungs.* London: Nelson, 1965.
Flowers, Stephen E. "Revival of Germanic Religion in Contemporary Anglo-American Culture." *Mankind Quarterly,* 21:3 (1981), pp. 279-294.

Flowers, Stephen E. "Toward an Archaic Germanic Psychology." *Journal of Indo-European Studies*, 1:1-2 (193), pp. 117-138.
———————. *Runes and Magic: Magical Formulaic Elements in the Older Tradition*. New York: Lang, 1986.
———————. *The Galdrabók: An Icelandic Grimoire*. York Beach, ME: Weiser, 1988.
Gennep, Arnold van. *The Rites of Passage*. trs. M.B. Vizdom and G.L. Caffee. Chicago: University of Chicago Press, 1960.
Goodrick-Clarke, Nicholas. *The Occult Roots of Nazism: The Ariosophists of Austria and Germany 1890-1935*. Wellingborough, UK: Aquarian, 1985.
Grimm, Jacob. *Teutonic Mythology*. tr. S. Stallybrass. New York: Dover, 1966, 4 vols. (first published 1835).
Grønbech, Vilhelm. *The Culture of the Teutons*. London: Oxford University Press, 1931, 2 vols.
Höfler, Otto. *Kultische Geheimbünde der Germanen*. Frankfurt/Main: Diesterweg, 1934
Hollander, Lee M., trans. *The Poetic Edda*. Austin: University of Texas Press, 1962.
Jacobi, Jolande. *The Psychology of C.G. Jung*. New Haven: Yale University Press, 1973 [1942].
Jacobsen, Lis and Erik Moltke. *Danmarks Runeindskrifter*. Copenhagen: Munksgaard, 1941.
Jones, Gwen. *A History of the Vikings*. London: Oxford University Press, 1984, 2nd ed.
———————, tr. *Erik the Red and other Icelandic Sagas*. Oxford: Oxford University Press, 1961.
Jung, Carl. *The Archetypes and the Collective Unconscious*. (=Bollingen Series 20, vol. 9 pt. 1 of the Collected Works) tr. R.F.C. Hull. Princeton: Princeton University Press, 1959.
Kummer, Siegfried Adolf. *Heilige Runenmacht*. Hamburg: Uranus-Verlag, 1932.
———————. *Runen-Magie*. Dresden: K. Hartmann, 1933.
———————. *Rune-Magic* tr. E. Thorsson. Austin: Rûna-Raven, 1993.
List, Guido von. *The Secret of the Runes*. Translated by Stephen E. Flowers. Rochester, VT: Destiny Books, 1988.
Littleton, C. Scott. *The New Comparative Mythology: An Anthropological Assessment of the Theories of Georges Dumézil*. Berkeley: University of California Press, 1973, 2nd ed.
Mallory, J. P. *In Search of the Indo-Europeans: Language, Archaeology and Myth*. London: Thames & Hudson, 1989.
Marby, Friedrich Bernhard. *Runenschrift, Runenwort, Runengymnastik* Vol. 1/2, *Marby-Runen-Bücherei*. Stuttgart: Marby Verlag, 1931.
———————. *Marby-Runen-Gymnastik* Vol. 3/4, *Marby-Runen-Bücherei*. Stuttgart: Marby Verlag, 1932.
———————. *Rassische Gymnastikals Aufrassungsweg*. Vol 5/6, *Marby-Runen-Bücherei*. Stuttgart: Marby Verlag, 1935.
———————. *Die Rosengarten und das ewige Land der Rasse*. Vol. 7/8, *Marby-Runen-Bücherei*. Stuttgart: Marby Verlag, 1935.
Miller, David L. *The New Polytheism: Rebirth of the Gods and Goddesses*. New York: Harper and Row, 1974.
Morris, William, tr. *Volsunga Saga*. Introduction and glossary by Robert Gutman. New York: Collier, 1962.
Mundal, Else. *Fylgjemotiva i Norrön Literatur*. Oslo: Universitetsforlaget, 1974.
Osborn, Marijane, and Stella Longland. *Rune Games*. London: Routledge and Kegan Paul, 1982.

Otto, Rudolf. *The Idea of the Holy.* tr. J.W. Harvey. Oxford: Oxford University Press, 1958.
Page, R.I. *Introduction to English Runes.* London: Methuen, 1973.
Polomé, Edgar C. "Some Comments of 'Völuspá' Stanzas 17-1." In: *Old Norse Literature and Mythology: A Symposium,* ed. E. C. Polomé. Austin: University of Texas Press, 1969.
——————. "The Indo-European Component in Germanic Religion." In: *Myth and Law among the Indo-Europeans: Studies in Comparative Indo-European Mythology.* ed. J. Puhvel. Berkeley: University of California Press, 1970.
——————. "Approaches to Germanic Mythology." In: *Myth in Indo-European Antiquity.* Berkeley: Univestity of California Press, 1974.
Robinson, Orrin W. *Old English and its Closest Relatives: A Survey of the Earliest Germanic Languages.* Stanford, CA: Stanford University Press, 1992.
Schneider, Karl. *Die germanischen Runennamen.* Meisenheim: Anton Hain, 1956.
Simpson, Jacqueline., ed. and tr. *Icelandic Folktales and Legends.* Berkeley: University of California Press, 1972.
——————, ed. and tr. *Legends of Icelandic Magicians.* Ipswich: D.S. Brewer, 1975.
Steblin-Kaminskij, M.I. *The Saga Mind.* trans. K.H. Ober. Odense: Odense Universitetsforlag, 1973.
Sturluson, Snorri. *The Prose Edda.* Tr. A. Brodeur. New York: American Scandinavian Foundation, 1929.
Tacitus, Cornelius. *The Agricola and the Germania.* tr. H. Mattingly. Harmondsworth: Penguin, 1948.
Thorsson, Edred. *Futhark: A Handbook of Rune Magic.* York Beach, ME: Weiser, 1984.
——————. *Runelore: A Handbook of Esoteric Runology.* York Beach, ME: Weiser, 1987.
——————. *At the Well of Wyrd: A Handbook of Runic Divination.* York Beach, ME: Weiser, 1988
——————. *Rune Might: Secret Practices of the German Rune Magicians.* St. Paul, MN: Llewellyn, 1989.
——————. *A Book of Troth.* St. Paul, MN: Llewellyn, 1989.
——————. *The Nine Doors of Midgard.* St. Paul, MN: Llewellyn, 1991.
——————. *Northern Magic.* St. Paul, MN: Llewellyn, 1992.
——————. *Rune-Song: A Practical Guide to Rune-Galdor.* Austin: Rûna-Raven, 1993.
Turville-Petre, E.O.G. *Myth and Religion of the North.* New York: Holt, Rinehart and Winston, 1964.
Valfells, Sigrid and James E. Cathey. *Old Icelandic: An Intorductory Course.* Oxford: Oxford University Press, 1981.
Vries, Jan de. *Altgermanische Religionsgeschichte.* Berlin: de Gruyter, 1956-57, 2 vols.
——————. *Altnordisches etymologisches Wörterbuch.* Leiden: Brill, 1961.
Webb, James. *The Occult Establishment.* La Salle, IL: Open Court, 1976.
Williams, Mary. *Social Scandinavia in the Viking Age.* New York: MacMillan, 1930.
Zoller, Robert. *Skaldic Number-Lore.* Austin: The Rune-Gild, 1986.
——————. *Towards a Germanic Esoteric Astronomy.* Austin: The Rune-Gild, 1986.

www.ingramcontent.com/pod-product-compliance
Lightning Source LLC
Chambersburg PA
CBHW030050100426
42734CB00038B/992